FRONTAL FACES
IN ATTIC VASE PAINTING
OF THE
ARCHAIC PERIOD

FRONTAL FACES
IN ATTIC VASE PAINTING
OF THE
ARCHAIC PERIOD

BY

YVONNE KORSHAK

ARES PUBLISHERS, INC.
CHICAGO MCMLXXXVII

First Edition

Copyright © 1987

ARES PUBLISHERS, INC.
7020 NORTH WESTERN AVENUE
CHICAGO, ILLINOIS 60645

ISBN 0-89005-448-7

ACKNOWLEDGMENTS

The author gratefully acknowledges that this project has benefited from the interest of J.K. Anderson and D.A. Amyx, University of California, Berkeley; Louise Berge, the Art Institute of Chicago; Patricia Lawrence, University of Louisiana, Baton Rouge; A.N. Oikonomides, Ares Publishers and Karl Schefold, University, Basle. The support they have offered through stimulating discussion, scholarly information and editorial assistance is deeply appreciated. The assistance rendered by other scholars in connection with specific problems encountered in the course of this research is indicated in the notes, and their help is acknowledged with deep appreciation. I would also like to express my sincere thanks to Irenè Aghion, Bibliothèque Nationale, Paris; Jean Balty, Musées Royaux d'Art et d'Histoire, Brussels; Ann Birchall, the British Museum; John Boardman, Ashmolean Museum; Pierre Devambez, Louvre Museum; Barbara Philippaki, National Museum, Athens; Martin Robertson, Ashmolean Museum; N. Roncalli, Vatican Museums and Anna Talochini, Archaeological Museum, Florence for exceptional courtesies offered in my study of Greek vases in their museums. I also owe thanks to many kind people who furnished me with photographs pertinent to my research. I would also like to express my gratitude to the members of my family who have encouraged me in this project.

CONTENTS

Acknowledgements . . . . *v*

Text 1

List of Frontal Faces:
    Satyrs: (BF) 45-51; (RF) 51-54. **Komasts, Symposiasts:** (BF) 54-55; (RF) 55-58. **Combat Figures:** (BF) 58-60; (RF) 60-63. **Palaestra Figures:** (BF & RF) 64. **Centaurs:** (BF & RF) 65. **Maenads:** (BF & RF) 65. **Muses:** (BF) 66. **Nereid:** (RF) 66. **Deities and a Titan:** (BF) 66; (RF) 67. **Female:** (Misc. RF) 67-68. **Male:** (Misc. BF) 68; (Misc. RF) 68-69.

Addendum 70

Index of Artistic Reference:
    Artist, Group and Class Names 73

Index of Collections 76

Illustrations 79

FRONTAL FACES
IN ATTIC VASE PAINTING
OF THE
ARCHAIC PERIOD

εἰ μὴ γὰρ Διονύσῳ πομπὴν ἐποιοῦντο καὶ
ὕμνεον ᾆσμα αἰδοίοισιν, ἀναιδέστατα εἴργαστ' ἄν·
ὡυτὸς δὲ ᾿Αίδης καὶ Διόνυσος, ὁτέῳ μαίνονται καὶ ληναΐζουσιν.

Heraclitus Fr. 15, Clement Protrepticus 34.

Throughout the Archaic period, when the most characteristic type of free-standing sculpture was the kouros, represented with rigid frontality from head to toe, Greek vase painters clung with few exceptions to the convention of depicting the face in strict profile, with the exception of the Gorgon who is always shown frontal (Illus. 1 & 49).[1] The intrinsic arresting effectiveness of the frontal face, taken together with its rarity, raises the question, do the occasional frontal faces occur at random, or can they be linked with an iconographical pattern? In order to address this question, examples of frontal faces in Attic vase painting of the Archaic period were searched for and collected and the present discussion is based upon an analysis of the *List* given below.

1. The frontal view of the head was fundamental for sculpture in the round, the profile view for vase painting and relief sculpture, and the seeming convergence toward the end of the Archaic period is not the convergence of influence, but a shared tendency to modify earlier conventions and depart from the simpler presentations; for a critical consideration of the "law of frontality," see Otto J. Brendel, *Prolegomena to the Study of Roman Art,* 1979, 65 ff. and passim.

The earliest representations of the Gorgon in Greek vase painting are in Corinthian art, and its tradition (not that of the

1

Two scholars have published material, in the past, on frontal faces in Greek vase painting based upon collected lists. Moritz Hoernes and Adolf Greifenhagen both recognized an element of pathos in the frontal face, but their views of the material and its organization differ. Hoernes,[2] the first author to identify the frontal face as an issue in vase painting, was interested in its affective power and believed that it lay in its very rarity which is a formal analogue for extreme emotional and physical states. Collecting examples of frontal faces from Archaic black-figure through red-figure, he divided these into essentially three groups: A) dead, dying, and imperiled figures; B) physically burdened and strenuously active figures; C) spiritually burdened and inwardly moved figures. Greifenhagen,[3] in a significant excursus in his study of the development of the Archaic komos, derived the power of the frontal face from its origins in

1. (continued) Proto-Attic amphora from Eleusis) becomes dominant in Attic representations of the Gorgon and gorgoneia; Humfry Payne, *Necrocorinthia,* 1931, 79 ff. and 362; Roland Hampe, "Korfugiebel and Frühe Perseusbilder," AM 60-61, 1935-36, 269 ff.; J.D. Beazley, *The Development of Attic Black-Figure,* 1964, 14; G. Mylonas, *The Proto-Attic Amphora from Eleusis,* 1957. The gorgon head may appear in profile as part of another object, e.g., the gorgon shield of Ajax by Exekias, Vatican 344, amphora, *ca.* 530, P.E. Arias and M. Hirmer, *A History of Greek Vase Painting,* Tr. and rev. B.B. Shefton, 1962, Pll. 62, 63, XVII; Karl Schefold, *Götter-und Heldensagen der Griechen in der spätarchaischen Kunst* (Schefold GHG), 1978, fig. 332; cf. 229.
2. Moritz Hoernes, *Urgeschichte der bildenden Kunst in Europa,* 3rd ed., 1925, 590 ff.
3. Adolf Greifenhagen, *Eine attische schwarzfigurige Vasengattung und die Darstellung des Komos im VI. Jahrhundert,* 1929, 69ff.; cf. Emil Kunze, *Gnomon* 8, 1932, 120 ff.; R. Lullies, AM 65, 1940, 3, n. 1; José Dörig, Olof Gigon, *Der Kampf der Götter und Titanen,* 1961, 33 ff. See also Korshak, *The Ancient World* 10, 1984, 89 ff. Additions to the List of Frontal Faces will be welcomed by the author.

magical, "demonic" apotropaia. Tracing frontal faces back to early frontal lions, sphinxes, panthers, owls, sirens, and Gorgons, he put forth the view that in the sixth century, as artists had a growing desire to express spiritual and psychological aspects of existence, the earlier magical frontality was transformed to express intense emotions. Greifenhagen collected examples of frontal faces in all fabrics, but in contrast to Hoernes confined his list to examples in black-figure. He divided his examples into seven groups: 1) Dionysos and satyr masks; 2) Dionysos cult statues; 3) muses with syrinx or flute; 4) men in komos or symposium; 5) satyrs and centaurs; 6) men psychically-pained or physically strained; 7) man in cult activity. Of these, groups 3 through 6 represent the artistic attempt to represent an actual "living face" in vase painting which is the focus of the present study. Group 2 includes Dionysos on the François Vase (Illus. 56) but is not homogeneous since the other two entries in this group represent Dionysos masks on draped cult images. Group 7 consists of one example, on a pinax, Exekias' funerary plaque in Berlin (Illus. 11).

In addition to the published works, there are three unpublished studies of frontal faces. In a doctoral dissertation, *Das En Face in der griechischen Vasenmalerei*, Gerhard Müller expressed the view that frontal faces may have formal functions — to clarify action or to provide variety in a series — or they may express psychological isolation and self-absorption.[4] Andrée Conrad, in an M. A. thesis, *The Development of the Frontal Face and the Three-Quarter View in Attic Red-Figure Vase-Painting to the End of the Fifth Century*, looked at examples on an individual rather than on a

4. Diss. Universität Wien, 1951, noted by H. Kenner, *Weinen und Lachen in der griechischen Kunst*, 1960, 39 ff. My deep thanks to Gerhard Zechner and Gerhard Müller for providing me with the Müller dissertation.

generalizing basis, and offered interesting observations in the course of her review.[5]

The present study has benefited from the insights of all of these works. In addition, since the appearance of the pioneering studies of frontal faces by Hoernes and Greifenhagen, large numbers of vases have been published in many compendia, such as the *Corpus Vasorum Antiquorum* (CVA), and in numerous books and periodicals, and J.D. Beazley's books on Attic black-figure and Attic red-figure have appeared in their early and mature forms.[6] This has made it possible to collect a list that is both larger and more focussed than in the earlier studies, providing a broad basis for the observation of patterns that emerge. In the present study, parameters are limited to Attic vase painting of the Archaic period,[7] for a number of rea-

5. M. A. thesis, Institute of Fine Arts, New York, 1972. Conrad's work was called to my attention initially by Dietrich von Bothmer, and I am grateful to him and to Darryl Amyx and Mary B. Moore who also stressed its interest. I am appreciative to Peter von Blanckenhagen for his help in connection with my consultation of this thesis. Cf. Korshak, *Frontal Faces in Attic Vase Painting of the Archaic Period,* M.A. thesis, University of California, Berkeley, 1966. In *The Development of the Facing Head Motif on Greek Coins and Its Relation to Classical Art,* 1979, Katherine P. Erhart gives attention to frontal faces in vase painting, and makes pertinent observations.

6. J.D. Beazley, *Attic Black-Figure Vase-Painters,* 1956 (ABV); *Attic Red-Figure Vase-Painters,* second edition, 1963 (ARV[2]); *Paralipomena* [additions to the above], 1971 (Para.); Also, Lucille Burn and Ruth Glynn, *Beazley Addenda,* 1982 (BA).

7. J.D. Beazley's designations in ARV[2] are used as a foundation for determining which painters to include as "Archaic"; this involves problems in that later works by some Late Archaic vase painters are post-Archaic in date, and early works by "Early Classical" artists were made in the Archaic period; however, use of the widely known Beazley schema maintains intact the oeuvre of artists whose work is rooted in the Archaic period and falls mainly within it, and minimizes arbitrary inconsistency in what

sons. The Attic corpus is large, and while Attic artists were open to influences from other fabrics as well as other media, they also had their own iconographical as well as stylistic patterns and preferences, and thus the Attic vases form a unit that can be viewed with profit. By carrying the investigation to the end of the Archaic period (in contrast to Greifenhagen who included only black-figure), one can gain insight into changes that herald the introduction of a new period, the Early Classical. By the same token, although there are continuities between Archaic and Classical, there are significant differences in all aspects of artistic production, and by confining the investigation to the Archaic period, it is possible to perceive underlying patterns that tend to be diffused in the Classical period (in this the list differs from those of Hoernes, Müller and Conrad who included Classical material as well). Material of other periods, fabrics, and media has been kept in consideration.

Survey of frontal faces

Frontal faces in Attic vase painting of the Archaic period fall into two major groups: 1) satyrs, and a related group of komasts and symposiasts, and 2) combat victims and a related group of losing athletes. A number of examples, while not fitting directly into the major groups, may be related to them; in terms of these two groups, the number of true anomalies is small.

SATYRS

Satyrs with frontal faces appear in the same kinds of scenes, perform the same actions, and cavort in the

---

7. **(continued)** is still in most cases a matter of relative chronology. Where there is no designation by Beazley, I have made one on the basis of available evidence. I have noted Archaic period vases by Early Classical painters where relevant.

same postures as satyrs in profile: they are simply much less frequent. On an amphora of the Burgon Group an ithyphallic satyr follows a youthful Hephaistos riding a mule, in a Return of Hephaistos led by Dionysos (Illus. 2), and again on a hydria in Florence (Illus. 3). Both of these satyrs hold the head tilted to the side in a rhythmic complement to the angular gestures of their limbs; the tilt of the head, natural as it is for the cavorting satyr, could not be indicated by a profile view, and the desire to represent it is an important factor in the relatively large number of frontal-faced satyrs with tilted heads. The tilt of the head may be extended comically to the horizontal, as when the satyr rests his head on the back of the donkey with whom he is erotically engaged (FF88). While a frontal-faced satyr in the Return of Hephaistos may be found behind the donkey, as on a krater by Lydos (Illus. 4), he may also be found anywhere else in the Dionysiac train, including in close proximity to Dionysos, as on the other side of the same vase (Illus. 5). A neck-amphora in Boston is unusually rich in variety of figures, in the luxuriance of the vintage scene surrounding Dionysos and Ariadne, and in the number of frontal faces included on a single vase (FF 45-48).[8] One near the handle on the left side of ''A'' dances behind a maenad; another under the handle left of ''B'' runs with broad stride toward the treading table while in front of him a satyr carrying a large basket of grapes over his shoulder peers from under his burden toward the viewer (Illus. 6); another, far right on ''B'', turns to the viewer as he hoists himself onto a hanging vine. The figures of this vase have been attributed to the Manner of the Lysippides Painter while the

---

8. Considering their rarity, frontal faces (FF) occur in multiple numbers on many more vases than one might expect, as one can see from a perusal of the *List*, one seeming to suggest another.

pattern work has been attributed to the Affecter, an artist known to us through his figured scenes. In the light of this evident collaboration, it is interesting that the inventiveness of the Boston neck-amphora is totally different from the static and repetitive compositions of the Affecter; for example, on an amphora in Orvieto, 240 (FF 23-25), the compositional patterns of the two sides of the vase are nearly identical, and such mechanical arrangements characterize his other works. An unusually large number of frontal-faced satyrs have come down to us on vases by the Affecter (Illus. 7); perhaps in his case, the frontal face allowed the artist to introduce variety to his scenes without injecting physical energy that would have disturbed his characteristic formality, but, in general, formal variety is one of the less important reasons for the artists' use of frontal faces in Attic vase painting. On a neck-amphora in Orvieto by the Affecter, 1014, a satyr (FF 22) raises his hand toward his brow as he looks out in the gesture of "aposkopein," intrinsic to the satyr dance and effectively represented by use of the frontal face.[9] Derived from its association with the dance, it was carried over to a satyr amorously creeping up on a sleeping maenad, on the neck of a red-figured rhyton by the Brygos Painter (Illus. 8).

The finest of the black-figure vase painters, Exekias, represented on a funerary plaque one mourner among several in a procession, with his face turned directly toward the viewer, a dignified and arresting image that is deservedly very well known (Illus. 11).

9. Ines Jucker, *Des Gestus des Aposkopein*, 1956, 16 ff., esp. 20, Pl. 1.

10. Dietrich von Bothmer published the vase, "An Amphora by Exekias," *Bulletin du Musée Hongrois des Beaux-Arts* 28, 1966, 17 ff. See also Mary B. Moore, "Horses by Exekias," AJA 72, 1968, 357 ff.

Less well known through illustrations is the frontal-faced satyr painted on an amphora in Budapest (Illus. 9-10).[10] The satyr, cavorting with upraised arms, is where one would expect to find him, in the presence of Dionysos with his kantharos and ivy, with maenads, and with another satyr. The paunchy frontal-faced satyr is a humorous figure, and one can see clearly in him the artist's desire to represent naturalistically the over-fleshed, wrinkled belly. In the same naturalistic spirit, Exekias has also rendered the sagging breast muscles of the satyr. Exekias painted shortly before the problem of representing, with an organic continuity, the twist between the chest and hips had been seriously addressed. His frontal chest and profile belly and hips are within the drawing conventions of his day, but his naturalizing interest in anatomical details calls attention to the awkwardness of the convention, making it harder to accept than in more patterned work; the pressure to represent passages of anatomy naturalistically, which one sees clearly in Exekias' rendering, eventually leads to a more organically resolved representation.

In terms of iconography, the frontal-faced satyr and the frontal-faced mourner on the pinax seem unrelated. The satyr's presence is iconographically conventional. The mourner is without parallel in extant paintings of the period, although the small number of painted plaques that have come down to us must be borne in mind. The pinax, while contemporary with the earliest frontal-faced dying warriors in black-figure, seems independent of this vase painting iconography. Although funerary, Exekias' procession on the pinax, punctuated by the frontal face, anticipates processional groupings at the very end of the Archaic period when, as is discussed below, the deviation from the conventional profile suggests a movement toward psychological individuation. Here, as in other of its aspects, the work of Exekias seems to anticipate later art in its psychological dimensions. Indeed, the pinax goes beyond most later vase paintings in the quality of individuation expressed by the frontal face; here, by turning the face frontal, away from the representational norm, the artist conveys private grief, the isolation of loss.

In contrast to the crude face of the satyr, that of the mourner is elegant. The face of the satyr is broad with fat cheeks, while that of the mourner is narrower and has a higher forehead. The linear renderings are expressive of the contrasts: for example, in the satyr, the lines of the mouth and of the creases above it are angular and very irregular while those of the mourner are full, round and smooth (a contrast that cannot be accounted for by the use of incision in the black-figure vase because for other kinds of figures Exekias' incised line is as smooth as that on the pinax). However, underlying the contrasts of expression and *facture* in these two frontal faces, one can see similarities beyond the use in both of a light wash to suggest greying hair. In the round eyes, circled pupils, the complex rendering of the frontally viewed mouth and in the relation of beard to chin one can recognize in each the same structural concepts.

The continuity of motifs between black-figure and red-figure vase painting can be seen in comparing the amphora of the Burgon Group (Illus. 2) with a cup in Laon in the Manner of the Epeleios Painter, with satyrs and donkeys (Illus. 12-13). Neither Hephaistos nor Dionysos is anywhere in sight on the cup; because of humorous and erotic associations, the donkey, borrowed from earlier representations, has found a place among satyrs and maenads independent of its links with the Return of Hephaistos. This comparison also demonstrates two contrasting modes by which the frontal face can be exploited for expressive

effect: the semiotic and the specific. As noted by
Hoernes, the impact of the frontal face can be the
result of the formal contrast it presents to the dominant profile view,[11] and in black-figure painting the
expressive power of the frontal face is often based
upon this simple and non-specific semiotic distinc-
tion. The facial expression of the frontal satyr on the
red-figure cup in the Manner of the Epeleios Painter is
very different, for it is specific, and would be recog-
nizable in any context: he faces us with a bold, glee-
ful, toothy grin. He is one of a number whose frontal
face may in part be attributed to the opportunity it
afforded the artist to represent a full smile; in this
frontal view there is a confrontation so direct it
takes on the character of a challenge. The unsymmetrical placement of the pupils adds to a tipsy effect,
although here the artist's intention is not certain.[12]

The formal contrast between frontal and profile
head remains a dominant expressive mode in red-
figure as it was in black-figure, but specific expressions of emotional states, such as that demonstrated
by the Laon cup, become more common in red-figure.
Some of the profile satyrs on the Laon vase also
smile: as the Archaic period unfolds, and artists' interest in observation of the world around them and in
psychology develops, they do not confine their inves-

11. A formal analysis of frontal and profile as semiotic in the
history of art, with meaning related in part to which view is stan-
dard and which deviant in a specific artistic style, is given by
Meyer Schapiro, "Words and Pictures," in *Approaches to
Semiotics* 11, 1973, Ch 4, 37 ff. Cf. Evelyn Radford, "Euphronios
and his Colleagues," JHS 35, 1915, 113, no. 17: "There is no attempt to render actual pain or fear . . . but the very rarity of the
full face serves to focus attention on it, and reserves for it, as it
were, a character other than that of the normal profile."
12. My appreciation of the element of challenge in the frontal
face was heightened by Conrad, who notes it in several
instances.

tigations of facial expression to the frontal view; however, we can see in viewing the satyrs on the Laon vase the expansion of artistic experience the frontal face offers in this area.

KOMASTS AND SYMPOSIASTS

These figures share with satyrs an association with wine and the activities and states of mind linked with it, and thus, as Greifenhagen recognized, their frontal-faced representation is derived from an affinity with satyrs. On black-figure vases, there are several frontal-faced komasts who dance erotically and with the same exaggerated gestures of satyrs, as on a neck-amphora Copenhagen (Illus. 14-15), and on another in Munich (Illus. 16). However, while the series of satyrs is continuous, the black-figure komasts are all early;[13] we have no frontal-faced komasts by the Affecter who, as noted, painted frontal-faced satyrs relatively often. The only frontal-faced reclining symposiast in Attic black-figure known to me is the one on the shoulder of the dinos in the Louvre (Illus. 17). Toward the end of the sixth century, however, as artists turn their attention more and more to scenes of everyday life, the subject of symposiasts and of komasts is enthusiastically taken up. Perhaps the earliest frontal-faced symposiast in red-figure is that by Euphronios on the krater in Munich (Illus. 18): as the bearded drinker reclines among friends, leaning on a striped cushion, he raises the cup to his lips so that, as often in this motif, the lower part of his face is covered by the cup, his moustache visible above the rim. It is surprising to realize that one has to reach back to the small figure

13. John Boardman, *Athenian Black Figure Vases* (Boardman ABV), 1974, 210, notes this extended period with few depictions of symposiasts.

on the Louvre dinos to find an earlier one like him.[14]
The hetaira drinking in a similar posture with her
friends on Europhronios' psykter in Leningrad (Illus.
19) is the only female frontal-faced drinker known to
me in Archaic vase painting. The reclining frontal-
faced symposiasts in Attic vase painting do not proffer
their cups to the viewer, as does Caravaggio's *Bacchus*
leaning on an elbow and looking directly at the viewer over two millennia later (Illus. 20),[15] but in the conjunction of the raised wine cup and the eyes peering
directly toward us over it, there is a similar note
of invitation.

The ready visual connection between satyrs and
komasts can be seen in the motif in which the frontal
face of a male figure, a satyr by Phintias (Illus. 21), a
komast by the Pedieus Painter (Illus. 22), provides a
medallion-like background for the profile of the female each embraces. Since these vignettes are so similar, and the former is on an amphora, the latter in the
tondo of a cup, we can note here that vase shape or
the placement of a scene on a vase is not related to the
employment of a frontal-face motif, although in some
cases compositions may be manipulated slightly to
harmonize well with a specific field. We have noted
that red-figure artists may convey specific emotions
through the frontal face. It is sometimes difficult to
judge how far this idea may be carried, and how
specific a state of mind can be imputed to a particular
face. There is some ambiguity but the interpretation
by François Villard of an ''expression of lust on [the]

14. Phineus appears frontal-faced as a symposiast on a black-
figure Chalcidian cup, Würzburg 164, *ca.* 530, Andreas Rumpf,
Chalkidische Vasen, 1927, Pll. 40 ff.; Schefold GHG, fig. 232; cf.
fig. 17.
15. Rudolf Wittkower, *Art and Architecture in Italy 1600-1750*, 2[d]
ed., 1965 Pl. 7 A; the *Bacchus* of *ca.* 1595 is in the Uffizi Gallery
in Florence.

tormented features" of this frontal-faced satyr by Phintias is a compelling one;[16] playful or rapturous expressions of lust are, however, more common.

The visual link between satyr and komast can be seen in the work of Douris who on occasion uses nearly identical motifs for each. A satyr on his cup in Harvard's Fogg Museum (Illus. 23) looks toward the viewer and waves while moving toward the left, like a komast on a cup in Boston (Illus. 24) who, however, does not tilt his head. The wave, seen here and elsewhere in conjunction with frontality, suggests that the viewer can join the party, and supports what Schapiro calls the "I-You" relationship of the frontal face.[17] The frontal view also offered artists the possibility of depicting the making of an utterance. The mouth of Douris' komast (although not that of the satyr) is open and he is probably singing. In other contexts, the frontal face with an open mouth may express a shock or pain, slackness of jaw or a cry, perhaps both, as on the warrior falling between Achilles and Memnon on the cup by the Brygos Painter (Illus. 25), or the one who falls alone in the tondo of a cup in the Villa Giulia (FF 185). On a cup in Copenhagen (Illus. 26), the open mouth is used to depict graphically a symposiast vomiting. When the pose of a komast or of a symposiast is not directly parallel with that of a satyr, artists may represent the figures in such a way as to foster the visual connection. For example, satyrs do not characteristically recline on couches like symposiasts, but vase painters often arrange a fillet around a drinker's head so that the loops at the side suggest a satyr's upraised ears, as for example on the

16. Jean Charbonneaux, Roland Martin, François Villard, *Archaic Greek Art*, 1978, 331.
17. Schapiro, 38 f.; the grammatical terminology is consistent with the structuralist approach to art applied in the essay.

cup by the Foundry Painter in Boston (FF 138). Komasts or symposiasts may be either bearded men or
beardless youths, but when these are grouped together, in almost every instance it is a bearded figure
who is represented with frontal face, evidently by
analogy with satyrs who are always bearded.[18]

COMBAT FIGURES

The frontal-faced fallen warrior enters Attic vase
painting later than does the frontal-faced satyr, the
first examples coming from near the beginning of the
last quarter of the sixth century. On an amphora in
London (Illus. 27), Eurytion falls frontal-faced while
the battle between Herakles and Geryon rages above
him. The victim's position, in which he has fallen
backward and supports himself on an elbow, is similar to that of the warrior fallen between Achilles and
Memnon on a neck-amphora in Brussels of the Three-
Line Group (FF 148). In contrast, the frontal-faced
warrior on the neck-amphora by the Swing Painter in
Brussels falls in the *knielauf* posture while two others
fight above his head (Illus. 28). The posture of a warrior fallen before a quadriga, on a neck-amphora in
Munich, is similar (Illus. 29). In general, in subsequent vase painting, warriors fall like these onto a

18. The association of the frontal face and the beard has been
noted, cf. Paul Jacobsthal, *Die melischen Reliefs*, 1931, 45, notes.
Erhart commenting on the difficulty of rendering the area of
chin and neck states that the full beard is a "general remedy for
an inadequate perspective technique," 84 ff. This may have
been a factor, but the presence of frontal-faced bearded satyrs
and the virtual absence of beardless ones (there are a few profile
beardless boy-satyrs, cf. FF 96) would have been an important
visual influence. For a fine, beardless face shown frontal see the
youth, perhaps Dionysos' son, Oinopion, with Dionysos in the
tondo of a cup by the Triptolemos Painter (Illus. 94), and there
are others.

bent knee, and the upper part of the body remains partially upright, whether the figure falls forward, like the warrior between Achilles and Memnon on the cup in Tarquinia by the Brygos Painter (Illus. 25), or backward, as on a cup in Berlin by Douris (Illus. 30). The position of the frontal-faced corpse of Achilles, supported nearly upright, is unique (Illus. 32); it may reflect the influence of illustrated wrestling holds (Illus. 40).

Several giant victims are represented with face frontal. An early example is Enkelados falling before Athena on a neck-amphora in Tours near the Red-Line Painter (FF 149). Alkyoneus smiles in his sleep as Herakles moves forward to kill him on a cup in Melbourne by the Nikosthenes Painter (Illus. 33), the sweet dreams suggested by his smile an ironic contrast to the imminent slaughter. Here, the frontal face offered the opportunity to depict in some detail the tightly closed eyes with eye lashes pressed close to the lids. Perhaps, following Bernard Andreae's interpretation, the giant's expression can be understood as malicious as well as humorous, and is thus part of a subtle characterization of personality, although as always with more complex readings of facial expression in Archaic vase painting, it is difficult to be certain.[19]

As representations of Theseus became frequent, reflecting the symbolic importance of his cult for Athens,[20] the youthful hero's antagonists Kerkyon and Skiron, like giants in being uncivilized and of great strength, are represented with faces frontal. Since Theseus fought with them bodily, they are shown

19. JdI 77, 1962, 177 ff. For the subject, 133 ff.; cf. Schefold GHG, 141 f.
20. For the symbolic meaning attributed to the Theseus cycle by the Alkmaeonids, and the effect on art, Schefold, *Wort und Bild,* 1975, "Kleisthenes," especially 74 f., GHG, 161 ff.

trapped or thrown in wrestling holds, as Skiron
appears thrown over the cliff, on a cup by Douris (Illus. 31), on another by the Kleophrades Painter (Illus.
34), and elsewhere. Oltos' representation of Herakles
wrestling with Nereus is unusual in that it is the hero
Herakles, not Nereus, who is shown with frontal face
(Illus. 35). The frontality of the combat victim is extended to moving representations of Astyanax, not
shown in any variation of the *knielaufschema* as are
true battling adversaries, but lying across the lap of
Priam, his head hanging down, on a hydria in Naples
by the Kleophrades Painter (Illus. 36), and, again with
face upside down, flung to his death by Neoptolemos
on a fragmentary cup in Berlin and the Vatican (FF
173).[21] On a cup in Perugia by Onesimos (Illus. 37),
Troilos is shown frontal-faced in front of the altar as
he tries to escape from Achilles who grasps his hair;
on a cup by Makron in Palermo he falls from his horse
(Illus. 38), the body of the horse a spectacular
demonstration of foreshortening. On one in the
Louvre by the Brygos Painter he is on horseback as
Achilles grabs him, again by the hair (Illus. 39). Like
Astyanax, Troilos although not a small child was a
youthful victim of the Greek victory, and these artists

21. Hermione Speier notes that the frontal face of Astyanax
helps to convey the full tragedy, "Die Iliupersisschale aus
Werkstatt des Euphronios," *Neue Beiträge zur klassischen Alter-
tumswissenschaft:* Festschrift Bernard Schweitzer, 1954, 113 ff.,
Pll. 21 ff. Cf. Radford, 114. For a reconstruction, and an attribution to Onesimos, see Dyfri Williams, "The Ilioupersis Cup in
Berlin and the Vatican," *Jahrbuch der Berliner Museen* 18, 1976, 9
ff., figs. 1 ff. The reconstruction published by Speier includes a
prone figure with frontal face (FF 173), based upon an un-
attached fragment of shoulder, hair and ear, and is included in
Williams' reconstruction. The position of the figure as
reconstructed and the angular torsion in the posture, greater
than in the figure of Astyanax, is uncharacteristic for the period,
and the figure may not be correctly reconstructed.

probably drew his face frontal through association with Astyanax, also shown slaughtered near an altar.[22]

PALAESTRA FIGURES

The association of victimization with frontality was extended to scenes in the palaestra, and in a number of representations of athletic contests, the losing figure is represented with face frontal. On an amphora in Munich, a wrestler is shown frontal-faced as he is lifted from the ground (Illus. 40), the partial overlapping of his face by his opponent's profile recalling the composition of embracing couples by Phintias and the Pedieus Painter (Illus. 21-22); on a stamnos in the Vatican by the Michigan Painter (Illus. 41), the disadvantaged wrestler is shown with face frontal.[23] Again, the Andokides Painter represents a wrestler, frontal-faced, lifted from the ground (Illus. 42).[24] Near the end of the Archaic period, on the outside of a cup in London, Douris represents a losing boxer falling to his knees (Illus. 43) in the same pose he uses for an armed and falling warrior in the tondo of another of cup (Illus. 44) (cf. Illus. 25) although in the tondo the figure is compressed somewhat to fit the round field. This interchanging of pose for military and athletic victims is parallel with what we have already noted between satyrs and komasts.

Among artists who represented frontal faces in the context of the palaestra was Onesimos. While in his depictions of victims such as Kerkyon and Troilos he sustains the link between the frontal face and

22. For the pictorial association of Astyanax and Troilos from the early sixth century, see Matthew I. Wienecke, "An Epic Theme in Greek Art," AJA 58, 1954, 293 f. and notes, 303.
23. JHS 25, 1905, 287 f., fig. 24.
24. For Panathenaic association, see Erika Simon, *Die griechischen Vasen* (Simon GV), 1976, 91 f., Pll. 81 ff.

                    YVONNE KORSHAK

defeat, he does not maintain this meaning in varied
palaestra scenes, and we can thus witness in this artist of the Late Archaic period a weakening of the
iconographical association between frontality and victimization. His cup in Munich (Illus. 45) is instructive
in this regard: if we were to look at only the wrestlers
about to grapple, we might surmise, given the association between frontality and defeat, that the artist was
informing us that the frontal-faced contender would
be the loser. This would be moving beyond the evidence since there are no other examples of the prolep-
tic use of frontality. Furthermore, there is no opponent in sight for the jumper with halteres, and the
leaning youth is for the moment *hors de combat.* On a
cup in Boston, the frontal face is transferred to a
boxer who seems to be wielding a telling blow (Illus.
46). Clearly Onesimos has dissociated here the frontal face from its earlier meaning. On his cup in the
Louvre, the frontal face of the boy washing himself
with a sponge may be related to scenes in the palaestra through the common locus (Illus. 47),[25] but the im-
plication of defeat is not present. Additional consideration of Onesimos' use of frontality will be reserved
until other examples of this artist's frontal faces are
examined below.

While on the surface the two groups of frontal-
faced figures seem unrelated except for their frontality, upon consideration it becomes apparent that
iconographical and iconological connections between
them do exist. On an iconographic level, both groups
are related to the quintessentially frontal image in
Greek art, the Gorgon, although for each, the connection with the Gorgon is of a different kind. Satyrs are

25. René Ginouvès identifies this scene with others as bathing
associated with the palaestra, *Balaneutikē,* 1962, 127 f., fig. 39.

linked with Gorgons through the idea of the mask, for each an essential attribute. Masks can be understood in formal and in functional terms; for the Archaic period, the formal character of gorgoneion[26] and satyr masks, as well as those of Dionysos, are well known through representations in vase painting and other media.[27] However, questions regarding the way masks were actually used in archaic Greece, particularly in their connection with performances, remain to be answered. Masked figures representing fertility spirits, most commonly recognized as satyrs, seem to have participated in Attica and elsewhere in Dionysiac festivals, in connection with danced mimetic performances that have been seen as important in the foundations of later Greek drama.[28] T.B.L. Webster has taken the point of view that figures wearing Gorgon masks figured importantly in early danced performances, drawing upon the evidence of terra-

26. For a comprehensive study of the formal development of the gorgon head in Greek art of the Archaic and later periods, see Josef Floren, *Studien zur Typologie des Gorgoneion,* 1977. My thanks to J.D. Belson for writing to me about this study.

27. Greifenhagen, 69, includes images of masked Dionysos idols as well as of Dionysos masks on vases on his list of frontal faces. The fundamental study is A. Frickenhaus, "Lenäenvasen," *72. Berline Winckelmannsprogramm,* 1912. For recent analysis, see Jean-Louis Durand and Françoise Frontisi-Ducroux, "Idoles, figures, images: autour de Dionysos," RA 1982, 81 ff. Cf. Evelyn Bell, "Two Krokotos Mask Cups at San Simeon," *California Studies in Classical Antiquity* 10, 1977, 1 ff. For the controversy over whether the festival indicated on the vases is the Lenaia, see Durand and Frontisi-Ducroux, 82; cf. T.B.L. Webster, *Greek Art and Literature 700-530 B.C.,* 1959, 65 f., and *The Greek Chorus,* 1970, 18 f., 81ff. Hetty Goldman touches on the masked Dionysos idols in "The Origin of the Greek Herm," AJA 46, 1942, 58 ff. For "detached" frontal-faced heads of Dionysos and satyrs on coins of the 6th century probably representing masks, Erhart, 77 ff.

cotta masks from the Sanctuary of Artemis Orthia near Sparta, and those from Tiryns.[29] While these terracotta masks are probably votive (although as Webster notes, they are large enough to be worn), they bring the mask from the flat representations in vase painting into the realm of three-dimensional objects that are indeed very suggestive of performance masks.[30] It should be noted that while the frontal faces of satyrs and Gorgons are linked through the idea of the mask underlying their representation, not all figures associated with masks are shown with frontal face. I know of only two representations of frontal-faced Dionysos in Attic vase painting (or in any other fabric) (Illus. 56 and 58) but his mask is well known in scenes in which it appears as part of a cult idol, and often appears as an independent motif on vases (Illus. 48). The mask is thus a contributing but not sufficient cause for frontal-faced representation.

An idea linking the other large group of frontal-faced figures, fallen victims, with the Gorgon is that like them, she is herself a victim of physical violence. Beheaded by Perseus' harpe, she falls as on the olpe

28. Karl Meuli, ''Schweizer Masken und Maskenbrauche,'' *Gesammelte Schriften,* 1, 1975, 254 ff.; Arthur Pickard-Cambridge, *Dithyramb, Tragedy and Comedy,* 2d ed., revised by Webster, 1962, 69 ff. and passim; Webster, *Greek Art and Literature,* 55 ff., and *The Greek Chorus,* 11 ff. and passim; Schefold GHG, 8, *Wort und Bild,* 34 ff.
29. R.M. Dawkins, ed., *The Sanctuary of Artemis Orthia at Sparta,* 1929, Pl. 56, 2-3 (gorgon masks); Pl. 56, 1 (satyr-looking mask); cf. *Dithyramb, Tragedy and Comedy,* Pl. 12, for illustration of gorgon mask from Tiryns, no. 69 on p. 310 for bibliography; Webster, *Greek Art and Literature,* 75, no. 28, also points to the Proto-Attic amphora from Eleusis, while noting that the ''mask-like face may be an idiosyncracy of the painter.'' See also the described views of Meuli, 2, 1044, ff. concerning a dance and mask festival associated with the Artemis Orthia sanctuary; cf. Walter Burkert, *Homo Necans,* transl. Peter Bing, 1983, 170 f., 235 ff.

by the Amasis Painter of *ca.* 540 B.C.,[31] and on a later hydria by the Antimenes Painter in the Villa Giulia, *ca.* 520 B.C. (Illus. 49), in the *knielaufschema,* a posture that can convey both the idea of collapse and of flight. Medusa, the Gorgon victim, with her knees bent and face frontal offered a victim type for representations of the battle victim falling to his knees with face turned to the front, as on the neck-amphora by the Swing Painter (Illus. 28, and others). The essentially derivative nature of the frontal-faced warrior victim is indicated by the lateness of entry of the motif into the repertory, and the small number of black-figure examples.

It has been suggested that the introduction of frontal-faced falling warriors into black-figure in this period may reflect the influence of monumental sculpture, specifically the frontal-faced giants in the Gigantomachy on the Siphnian Treasury frieze,[32] and it is natural to think of these powerful figures in terms

30. A cup in the Vatican, 335, ABV 57, 111, by the C Painter, *ca.* 560, Carlo Albizatti, *Vasi antichi dipinti del Vaticano,* IV, Pll. 34 and 36, with Gorgons and satyrs, may offer pictorial evidence for Gorgons in early performances. Obverse: a Gorgon, Athena, Hermes and Perseus; reverse: a Gorgon between two satyrs; cf. Beazley, "Prometheus Fire-Lighter," AJA 43, 1939, 624 f., Frank Brommer, *Satyrspiele,* 1944, 74 (nr. 36), 82 (nr. 173). Pictorial evidence for a ceremony involving women, perhaps in a circle or a semi-circle, and possibly masked may be given by a fragment of a Corinthian pyxis found in the excavations of the Sanctuary of Demeter and Kore on Acrocorinth during the summer of 1965, C-65-38, *Hesperia* 37, 1968, Pl. 91 d, p. 320. The fragment includes two women in profile who extend their arms toward a central woman, depicted frontal-faced; to the right of the woman on the right is the inscription "Hera." I am grateful to D. Amyx and R. Stroud for informing me of this fragment at the time it was excavated.
31. London B 471, 540-530 B.C., ABV 153, 32; Para 64. Boardman ABV, fig. 80; Schefold GHG, fig. 95.
32. Conrad, 36.

of influence in this connection. There is a certain spiritual kinship between the giants and the victims on the vase paintings. However, neither of the giants falls in the *knielaufschema;* one lies completely on his side facing the viewer;[33] the position of the other attacked by Cybele's lion[34] more nearly approaches the *knielaufschema* since his knees are bent and his face is *nearly* frontal (oblique however to the frontal "picture plane") but the thrust of the attack comes below his head, not above as in the *knielaufschema,* diffusing somewhat the visual relation to that posture. The frontal-faced black-figure fallen combattants in Brussels (Illus. 28), Munich (Illus. 29), and Tours (FF 149) fall in the *knielaufschema.* In the depictions of Eurytion in London (Illus. 27), and the fallen Homeric warrior in Brussels (FF 148), the victims, while in a more extended position, do not lie on the ground, but bend their knees and hold the upper part of their bodies supported on their elbows, a bent body posture that is related to the *knielaufschema* (and may be developed through a synthesis of it with the general reclining symposiast position). Since the posture of the black-figure warriors is more like that of the Gorgon as depicted in vase painting than that of the sculptured Giants, it is plausible to see the introduction of frontal-faced fallen warriors in black-figure vase painting as a development within the medium, bearing in mind always that the boundaries between media are never completely sealed. The *knielaufschema* continues to underlie the position of frontal-faced fallen warriors in red-figure, although it is modified in a naturalistic direction (Illus. 25, 30, 44).

Secondary interactions between the frontal-faced fallen warrior and other frontal-faced types can be

33. Charbonneaux *et al.,* fig 204; Schefold GHG, fig. 68/69.
34. Charbonneaux *et al.,* fig. 203. Schefold GHG, fig. 67.

observed. The helmet itself is mask-like, an artificial face that covers the real one, and this was probably a contributing factor in the use of the frontal face for defeated combattants. Indeed, exploiting the tension between the metallic outer face, the helmet, and the real one, visible only through the eyes peering from the mask-like shape of the eye-hole, artists expressed an effective pathetic contrast (Illus. 29). In a vignette from an Iliupersis (Illus. 50), behind the helmet of a fallen warrior one can see the eyes with the converging pupils of disorientation; like Patroclus, ''στρεφεδί-νηθεν δὲ οἱ ὄσσε.'' (Homer *Iliad* XVI. 792).[35] In work by Douris, the raised helmet cheek pieces flanking the frontal, bearded faces of fallen warriors resemble satyrs' ears (Illus. 30 and 44), supporting a visual connection between these types.

In addition to having iconographical connections with the Gorgon, it can be recognized that both groups — satyrs and drunken revellers, and victims — are in a state of diminished control over the self. In recognizing a kind of coming together of opposites in frontality, this observation is related to the psychological interpretation of Greifenhagen, who believed that the early demonic frontal face came later to express intense emotions, first the joy of carousal and, later, pain and physical strain. However, in seeking to understand these groups in terms of what they have in common, the view that the significant factor is psychological intensity is insufficient. The feelings experienced by a warrior in the face of a brutal and ultimately overpowering physical attack may encompass intense emotions such as rage or despair, but the

35. Erhart's view, 73 and notes, can be fully accepted that what looks like a transverse helmet crest on warriors such as this is the depiction of ''a longitudinal crest on a frontal helmet.''

compass intense emotions such as rage or despair, but the experience of cloudy perception and dimming vision is at least as likely:

> πᾶν δέ οἱ ἐν χείρεσσιν ἄγη δολιχόσκιον ἔγχος,
> βριθὺ μέγα στιβαρὸν κεκορυθμένον· αὐτὰρ ἀπ' ὤμων
> ἀσπὶς σὺν τελαμῶνι χαμαὶ πέσε τερμιόεσσα.
> λῦσε δὲ οἑ θώρηκα ἄναξ Διὸς υἱὸς ᾿Απόλλων.
> τὸν δ' ἄτη φρένας εἷλε, λύθεν δ' ὑπὸ φαίδιμα γυῖα,
> στῆ δὲ ταφών

Homer *Iliad* XVI. 801 ff.

The experience of intoxication also eludes a single definition of psychological intensity, partaking as much of the numbing of perception as of its intensification. Furthermore, many intense emotions that one can postulate, notably the exultation of victory, regularly paired with depictions of defeat, are never represented by means of the frontal face.

The factor shared by the Archaic drunk and dying or defeated figures is not psychological but existential, since it can be defined not by the quality of their perceived experience, but rather by their position in the continuum of human will and action. What drunken and dying figures have in common is that particular relationship between mind and body, marginal in Greek culture and in western civilization in general, in which governance of the self is relinquished, and nature takes hold. In this sense they are "demonic." This state of being *may* be one of extreme psychological intensity, hence the "pathos" often associated with the frontal face, and central in the views of Hoernes and Greifenhagen. It also provides a context for another very different psychological state, that of self-absorption noted by Müller, obviously appropriate for describing Classical figures such as the frontal-faced grieving Priam in the Departure of Hector by the Hector Painter,[36] but also relevant to the closing in of consciousness in the Archaic drunken and dying ones. For both satyr and dying warrior, limbs grow weak and consciousness dims, and they meet in an extreme state of being, the realm of lost control.

Other frontal faces

Although most of the frontal faces listed fall readily into one of the two main groups, a few do not. Since the focus of this paper is on the iconographic patterns that emerge from the collected corpus, and in these other cases we are dealing with few examples, it is not possible here to resolve the iconographical problems they raise, but some observations can be made.

There are five frontal-faced centaurs in the *List*, ranging in time from the second quarter of the sixth century to the end of the Archaic period (FF 207-211 and Illus. 51-54). Since they are so few, it is difficult to determine whether they are random anomalies or expressions of an underlying iconographical pattern. Greifenhagen, noting that centaurs have a psychological affinity with satyrs through their association with drunkenness, subsumes them within the same category. The resemblance between them is physical as well as psychological, in that both share horsy features and coarse faces and are generally seen as representing an uncivilized state. However, in spite of these similarities, the two types remain quite distinct

---

36. Vatican 16570, Korshak, ''Der Peleusmaler und sein Gefährte, der Hektormaler,'' AntK 23, 1980, Pll. 27, 2 and 4, 32,3. For the three-quarter view in this period expressing experience inwardly-turned, *ibid.*, 127, Pll. 31, 1-3. Cf. Paul Jacobsthal on frontal body posture expressing self-absorption, ''The Nekyia Crater in New York,'' *Metropolitan Museum Studies* 5, i, 1934, 117 ff. For a view somewhat aligned with the one offered in the present study, see recently F. Frontisi-Ducroux, ''Au miroir du masque,'' in *La Cité des Images*, 1984, 147 ff.

in Greek art and mythology. Centaurs do not share
the satyrs' privilege of serving Dionysos, nor do they
seem to have had a significant role in proto-dramatic
presentations. Once again, in considering centaurs,
evidence relating to the Gorgon must be noted since,
in the early period of Greek art when the forms of
hybrid monsters were still fluid and changing,[37] the
Gorgon was sometimes represented in the form of a
centaur, as on the neck of the relief pithos from Boeo-
tia in the Louvre with Perseus beheading Medusa
(Illus. 55), and connections between Medusa and centaurs have been postulated.[38] Provisionally, it seems
appropriate to interpret the few known frontal-faced
centaurs in Attic vase painting as lying within an iconographical tradition separate from that of satyrs,
perhaps with an indepenent link to the Gorgon by
way of the image of the hippomorphic Medusa.

The François Vase, in its volute-krater shape, and
in its rich depiction of myth and legend, initiates
many features seen in later Attic vase painting; however, its uses of frontality are not taken up by later
artists. Two figures on the François Vase are shown
with frontal face, Dionysos, and Kalliope playing the
syrinx (Illus. 56), the latter similar to the nearly con-

37. For early monster metamorphoses, Ernst Buschor, "Ken-
tauren," AJA 38, 1934, 128 ff.
38. Louvre CA 795. Jörg Schäfer, *Studien zu den griechischen
Reliefpithoi des 8.-6. Jahrhunderts v. Chr. aus Kreta, Rhodos, Tenos
und Boiotien,* 1957, 73 (B2); Hampe, *Frühe griechische Sagenbilder
in Böotien,* 1936, Pll. 36, 38, pp. 56 f.; detail Schefold,
Frühgriechische Sagenbilder, 1964, Pl. 15 b. For the view that
Medusa is related to centaurs, Paul V.C. Baur, *Centaurs in
Ancient Art,* 1912, 99 f. nr. 240, 127, nr. 312; cf. A. De Ridder,
BCH 22, 1898, 448 ff., Pll. IV-V, for a rationalizing discussion
and examples on seals of the hippomorphic gorgon; cf.
Boardman, *Archaic Greek Gems,* 1968, "The Gorgon-horse
Group," 27 ff.

temporary frontal-faced muses on dinoi by Sophilos (Illus. 57). On the François Vase, Dionysos carries his gift to Thetis, a golden amphora, over his shoulder, and Beazley suggested that the frontal face can be related to the burden: "He hastens, almost stumbles forward, holding an amphora full of wine on his shoulder, wine for the feast . . . The god here, feeling the weight and effort, turns towards the spectator, almost as if for sympathy, a contrast to the easy, un-conscious bearing of the other deities." [39] However, the interpretation of the burdened god is question-able, both as a religious concept for the period, and visually, since with the upper part of his body upright, Dionysos seems to carry this amphora lightly, slipping the fingers of one hand through the handle, his other hand free. He looks far less bur-dened than the satyr lugging a wineskin in the Return of Hephaistos elsewhere on this vase,[40] or than the satyr weighed down by a load of grapes in a basket, on the neck-amphora in Boston (Illus. 6). Dionysos' stride is broad, and his legs are bent, but since he does not seem to feel the amphora as heavy, his posture may be a reflection of the dance often seen among satyrs in his train, and in which he is sometimes shown to participate;[41] the suggestion of dance in Dio-nysos' posture, through the link between dance and mimetic performances, supports Greifenhagen's insight that it may be the mask that has influenced this representation of a frontal-faced Dionysos which, however, one must bear in mind, is iconographically

39. Beazley, *Development*, 28. The amphora, made by Hephaistos, held the ashes of Achilles and Patroclus, *Odyssey* xxiv. 73 ff. Rumpf, rev. Beazley *Development*, *Gnomon* 25, 1953, 469 f.; Walter F. Otto, *Dionysos Mythos und Kultus*, 1960, 53.
40. Cf. a detail of a satyr bending beneath the weight of a wineskin, Simon GV, Pl. 56 center, with the detail of Dionysos, Pl. 56, below.

anomalous; the only other example known to me is Dionysos seated, on a cup in Boulogne-sur-Mer (Illus. 58). What then of the muse Kalliope playing the syrinx on the François Vase, and the closely related frontal-faced figures on the dinoi by Sophilos? Although a unitary explanation of iconographical phenomena is always appealing, there is no evidence for an association of muses, or nysai, with masks. One can imagine that mimetic festivals which featured personalities such as Dionysos and satyrs may have included them, but this is speculation. As Max Wegner and others have observed, the syrinx gains intelligibility when seen from the front[42] (and covers the lower part of the face like a cup or beard as we have seen in later representations); frontal-faced satyrs play the auloi in later pictures (Illus. 59-63; cf. Komasts and Symposiasts, Illus. 64-66, and FF 118). However, like Dionysos, the frontal-faced female syrinx players are not represented in subsequent vases of the period.[43]

41. On the François Vase, Dionysos' front and back knees are clearly bent, and the breadth of his stride can be recognized in the fact that a line dropped directly down from the back of his head would not intercept the front of his back foot, as it would that of other figures in this procession. Dionysos appears to be in a decorous version of Webster's posture C, D, (k), *The Greek Chorus,* 3 f. For an early dancing Dionysos, the cup in Copenhagen, N. M. 5179, by the Heidelberg Painter, ABV 62, 64, 570-560 B. C., CVA 3, III H, Pl. 113, 3, cited by Webster, *ibid.,* 13. For a continuation of the tradition of the dancing Dionysos, Würzburg L 265 by the Amasis Painter, cf. FF 34, noted by Beazley, *Development,* 60 (although this is not the earliest). Cf. Simon's observation of Dionysos approaching an altar dancing on a red-figure kantharos in Boston by the Nikosthenes Painter, 00.334, CB iii, pl. 68, *Opfernde Götter,* Berlin, 1953, 51; cf. Martin Robertson, *A History of Greek Art* (Robertson *History*), 1975, 136.
42. *Das Musikleben der Griechen,* 1949, 59 f. Greifenhagen, 73, links the frontal face of the syrinx player to the idea of ugliness

In view of the relative frequency of frontal-faced satyrs, it is surprising that there are only three frontal-faced maenads, all from near the end of the Archaic period. In a panel scene on the shoulder of a kalpis by the Kleophrades Painter, a maenad (FF 213) dances in the presence of two other dancing maenads, a satyr who leans his back against a cushion as he accompanies them on the auloi, and Dionysos. Through the rendering of her birded sleeves and outstretched arms, tilted head, and hair (painted in dilute glaze) streaming loosely, the artist conveys a moment of abandon. As Beazley indicated, this maenad seems to throw her head back, yet the lower part of her face is disproportionately long; in an accurately fore-shortened view of the head from below the vertical picture space of the lower part of the face would be diminished, not as here lengthened.[44] Against the background of this experiment with this pose, it is exciting to recognize the mastery demonstrated by the Antiphon Painter ten or fifteen years later in drawing a male figure, possibly a satyr, with his head thrown back (Illus. 67): the mouth, nostrils and nose and eyes are visible and vertically compressed, the forehead is

42. **(continued)** and animality, through the ugliness associated with flute-playing (Athena throwing away her flute when she saw her reflection, Alkibiades' refusal to play it because it was disfiguring); however, as Erhart points out, 285 f., it is difficult to think of Kalliope as anything but beautiful. Müller and Conrad stress the usefulness of the frontal face for clarifying action.
43. For frontal females playing the auloi in relief metalwork, see the Argive shield bands, *ca.* 540, in Lullies, "Griechische Kunstwerke Sammlung Ludwig, Aachen, Eine Auswahl Austellung im Hessischen Landesmuseum Kassel, 1968," *Aachener Kunstblätter des Museumsvereins* 37, 1968, 135 ff.; cf. Schefold GHG, 67, fig. 80, cf. fig. 79.
44. "A Hydria by the Kleophrades Painter," AntK 1, 1958, 6, Pll. 2-4, 5, 7-8. Webster suggests the frontal-faced maenad may be "inspired by a member of a maenad chorus," *Monuments Illustrating Tragedy and Satyr Play*, 2d ed., 1967, 44 f., nr. AV1, 45.

lost to view. This representation is uniquely localized
in this period, and to my knowledge one has to turn to
Florentine art of the mid-fifteenth century for a com-
parable depiction; here, the St. Jerome of Castagno
provides a well known example of the motif (Illus.
68), and while the rendering of St. Jerome is more
anatomically concentrated, it is less radical in that
less of the saint's face is lost to view. [45]

On the fragment of a kylix in the Manner of the
Foundry Painter (FF 214), a maenad with face frontal
is carried off by a satyr and embraced by another, and
on a late black-figure cup of the Leafless Group (FF
212) a frontal-faced maenad appears with Dionysos,
satyrs and another maenad in profile. One can
surmise that these maenads owe their frontal faces to
their role as companions of satyrs, but there seems to
have been no pattern of representing maenads
frontal-faced as there was for satyrs. That these three
examples occur near the end of the period is linked
with the breaking up of the conventions governing
the use of the frontal face at the time, a loosening of
iconographical patterns that can be seen in other
ways. [46] For example, we have already observed that
in palaestra scenes by Onesimos, the frontal face has
begun to lose the connotation of defeat it had carried
in scenes of combat and contest.

45. For the visual connection with the Renaissance, cf. Erwin
Bielefeld, *Von griechischer Malerei*, 1949, 11. The foreshortened
view of the head seen from below becomes a virtuoso vogue in
mid-fifteenth century Renaissance Florence, and while it is
intriguing to consider that the brilliant drawing on this fragment
may have played a role in this development, I have not been able
to determine this. As Michael Vickers noted, the influence of
Greek vase painting on Italian Renaissance art has been
underestimated, ''A Greek Source for Antonio Pollaiuolo's *Battle
of the Nudes* and *Hercules and the Twelve Giants*,'' *The Art Bulletin*
59, 1977, 182 ff.

At the end of the Archaic period, the Berlin Painter added to the list of personae represented with frontal face new types of female figures: a Nereid fleeing in alarm at Peleus' pursuit of Thetis (Illus. 69); Nike (Illus. 70-72, and FF 227); and a woman fleeing from Poseidon (FF 233).[47] It would appear that in developing these new inventions, the Berlin Painter has borrowed from the image of the frontal-faced, running, female Gorgon, as in his own well known representation of her in Berlin;[48] like the Gorgon, Nikai are winged and move quickly, and like the Gorgon, the Nereid and the fleeing woman run in response to attack (cf. the alarmed woman, by the Brygos Painter, Illus. 73).[49] One recognizes in these new types the weakening of convention and the corollary broadening of the repertory of figures who might be represented with frontal face that we have already noted near the end of the Archaic period. However, even as artists pull away from the old iconographic patterns, these continue to exert their hold; although

46. For the development of Nikai by the Berlin Painter, Cornelia Isler-Kerényi, "Ein Spätwerk des Berliner Malers," AntK 14, 1971, 25 ff., Pl. 8,3 (Lon. E 513), Pl. 8,4 (Louvre G 199); the Basle Market Nike, same issue, adv. p. 1.
47. Lullies, "Der Dinos des Berliner Malers," AntK 14, 1971, 44 ff., Pl. 21,2 (Munich 8738), Pl. 22 (Taranto lekanis); for Poseidon and Amymone subject 54 and no. 64.
48. Munich 2312, amphora, ARV² 197,11, 1633, Para. 34,2; Boardman, *Athenian Red Figure Vases The Archaic Period* (Boardman ARV), 1975, fig. 153; studied by Beazley in relation to gorgoneia in AntK 4, 1961, 59, Pl. 25,2.
49. It should be noted that the Nikai of the Berlin Painter float rather than run as do earlier Nikai, cf. Isler-Kerényi, *Nike* 1969, 43 ff. The relative arrest is an element making possible the personal connection between the goddess and the viewer developed by the painter and eloquently described by Isler-Kerényi, AntK, *op. cit.*, 30. Cf. related frontal-faced figures by the Pan Painter of *ca.* 490, Oxford 312, ARV² 556,102, CVA Pl. 33,2, and his related frontal-faced Eros, Oxford 1920.58, fr., ARV² 556, 103, CVA Pl. 40,4.

Nike and the alarmed and running woman seem very different from satyrs and wounded warriors, the multidimensional image of the Gorgon in her many aspects, fleeing and falling, masked and frontal, appears to link them in their derivation.

The black-figure depiction of the squatting man stung by bees on an amphora in London (Illus. 80) may owe his frontal face to his discomfiture, as Greifenhagen indicates in placing him on his list in the group of strained and dying figures. The farcical treatment suggests a comic skit, and the frontal face may be connected with a mimetic, masked narrative.[50] The model for the posture is probably the type of squatting satyr known in examples of approximately the same period such as those in Berlin (Illus. 75-76) and in the Hearst Collection in San Simeon (Illus. 77-78); cf. FF 52-53. The type can be traced back early in the period (Illus. 74), and continues to the end of it (Illus. 79). The unique frontal-faced bellows-worker by the Foundry Painter also seems to squat (the lower part of his body is hidden by the kiln) (Illus. 81), and like a satyr he tilts his head (if he did not, we could not see him); his posture may be related to the same motif; the squatting satyr on a late black-figure cup fragment (Illus. 79) is approximately contemporary.[51]

The woman, fragmentary but frontal-faced, lying down in a scene of lovemaking (Illus. 82), and the Scythian resting (his mouth is open as if he is snoring)

50. For the view that the scene represents the theft of honey from the sacred bees, nurses of Zeus in Crete, see Arthur B. Cook, *Zeus*, 2, 1925, 928 f., Pl. 42; for Dionysiac associations of this scene, see C. Kerényi, *Dionysos*, transl. Ralph Mannheim, 1976, 30 ff. The subject is also known on an amphora by the Swing Painter, Basle, ex Züst, Para. 134, 21 *quater*.
51. The frontal faces of the models on the wall (frontal because artificial like masks) may have influenced the artist's use of the frontal face (cf. n. 8). See Greifenhagen, CVA Berlin 2, 26 for the heads on the wall as models.

(FF 241), probably owe their frontal faces in part to an association with reclining frontal figures such as Alkyoneus (cf. FF 229).[52] Because of her thin garment, and a certain boldness that seems to be projected here by the frontal view, the standing woman looking in the mirror on the cup in the Louvre by Douris is probably a hetaira (Illus. 83), one of the first depictions of a woman looking at herself in the mirror, a fundamental image of self-absorption, and one with a long and significant subsequent history. The mirror, next to her head, and the image it implies of the round isolated face may have suggested the frontal view to the artist who, as we have seen, made a number of frontal faces that can be understood more conventionally.[53]

In *The Birth of Athena* on the amphora in Richmond, both Athena and Zeus are shown with faces frontal (Illus. 84), a treatment that is unique for this subject,[54] and a hieratic representation of divinity that is uncharacteristic of Greek vase painting in general.[55] The massive-appearing frontal image of Zeus with Athena looks like a sculpture, and brings to mind the black-figure representation of a cult statue on a neck-amphora in London (Illus. 85).[56]

52. Cahn notes the relationship of this sleeping Scythian to frontal-faced depictions of sleeping Alkyoneus, *Münzen und Medaillen A. G., Sonderlist N.,* 1971, 58, nr. 74; there are a number of representations of Scythian symposiasts reclining and awake; the drinking horn and striped pillow suggest a symposium; see M. Vos, *Scythian Archers in Archaic Attic Vase-Painting,* 1963, 89 f., 126 f. (nrs. 417-425).
53. The round mirrored image of the face of Medusa as viewed by Perseus may have been in the back of the artist's mind in making this frontal face. Ginouves, 170, fig. 52, comments upon the earliness of this scene of a woman with her mirror.
54. Frank Brommer, "Die Geburt der Athena," JbMainz 8, 1961, Nachtrag, 83. On the earliest representation of the theme, on a relief pithos from Tenos, Tenos Museum, Zeus's face is frontal and Athena's is in profile, *ibid.,* 72; Schefold, *Frühgriechische Sagenbilder,* Pl. 13.

The depiction of Prometheus, frontal from head to toe, flanked by supporting Okeanids on the amphora in Munich is a portrait in ongoing passivity (Illus. 86). As such it forms a significant contrast to the defeated warriors and athletes who are the immediate victims of direct physical combat; however, there is a link with the other victims in the idea of helplessness, of lack of control which is so central in this highly original representation of Prometheus, and this may have been a factor in the artistic selection of the frontal face. The frontal standing symmetrical posture is without parallel among Archaic defeated warriors and athletes, but has a significant subsequent history.[57]

Four examples on three vases of frontal-faced helmeted figures are associated with a frontal quadriga, two charioteers and two warriors (the latter two on the same vase) (Illus. 88-89). There is a rich tradition of the frontal quadriga in sculpture that parallels that in vase painting.[58] In sculptural examples, the figures in the chariot are seen frontal-faced, as in the

55. Erhart, 279, notes the unusual hieratic presentation. The Potnia Theron on the Boeotian amphora in the National Museum in Athens, 5893, probably the earliest known frontal face on a humanoid figure in Greek vase painting, is a hieratic representation of divinity, but one which the Greeks did not maintain, Simon GV, 42 f., with bibliography, Pll. 16f., *ca.* 680 B. C. Edith Spartz, *Das Wappenbild des Herrn und der Herrin der Tiere in der minoisch-mykenischen und frühgriechischen Kunst*, 1962, 62 f., associates the deviations from frontality in these representations with a weakening of their religious significance. Chryssanthos Christou, *Potnia Theron*, 1968, 211 (nr. 1) dates the work to the early seventh century. The Gorgon appears as Potnia Theron on the Rhodian plate in the British Museum, A 748, Simon GV, 55 f., with bibliography, Pl. 32, *ca.* 630-610 B.C.; cf. Boardman's comments on the "familiar conception" of the Gorgon as Mistress of the Animals," *Archaic Greek Gems*, 30; cf. the views of Emil Kunze, "Zum Giebel des Artemistempels in Korfu," AM 78, 1963, 74 ff.

representations of the subject on the pediments of the Alkmaeonid Temple of Apollo at Delphi.[59] However, when vase painters depicted the scene, they did not often employ the frontal view of the face,[60] another indication of the vase painters' resistance to representing the frontal face, in spite of the possibilities it offered.

The regularity with which frontal faces are confined to two groupings throughout most of the Archaic period forms a background against which the weakening of the convention and the experimentation of artists at the end of the period can be seen. We have noted in Onesimos' palaestra scenes a tendency to dissociate the frontal face from the idea of defeat. The youth holding a hare in the tondo of the artist's cup in Boston (FF 242) is removed from any agonistic theme but there is probably a felt relation between the youth

55. (continued)
A human-looking frontal face appears earlier on a winged figure, probably a sphinx or siren, on a krater fragment from Pithekoussai, second half of the eighth century, Jeffery Klein, "A Greek Metalworking Quarter, Eighth Century Excavations on Ischia," *Expedition* 14, nr. 2, 1972, 38 f., figs. 5 and 6. This fragment also has on it the earliest signature, inscribed in retrograde, "...ινος μ'εποίεσε." In a context of Late Geometric decoration, the facing head, off-center in a metope field, is in outline, with eyes and nose represented as dots, the brow a straight line, the mouth a curved line, with double lines of hair falling to the shoulders on each side of a broad neck rendered in silhouette; much of a wing on the right and the tip of a wing on the left is preserved. A curved line outlined by dots (a branch?) is beyond the left wing tip.
56. London B 49, Schefold, "Statuen auf Vasenbildern," JdI 52, 1937, 38, Pl. 5.
57. Although the meaning is different, Prometheus' frontal posture, with elbows akimbo and arms and hands converging toward the face, is in structure related to that of frontal-faced players of the auloi or syrinx, cf. *supra*. Prometheus' posture also calls to mind Classical figures such as the passively supported

with his love gift and athletically involved young men on the exterior of the cup, one of which is shown with face frontal (Illus. 46). In the tondo of Onesimos' fragmentary cup in Oxford with school scenes (Illus. 91), an older man (lower left) dictates to a young man, while on the exterior, a youth leaning against a column is also shown with frontal face. We can see here the "neutral" frontal face of the palaestra extended to the school. The frontal face of the youth tuning his lyre (Illus. 92), seated before a teacher with a switch, seems due to the same link. On a pelike in Leningrad, a man merely listening to a music contest is shown frontal-faced (FF 248). The frontal face dissociated from victimization or drunkenness can be seen in few other vases toward the end of the Archaic period. In the zone

57. (continued)
frontal Andromeda on the hydria in London, E 168, Illus. 87, ARV² 1962, CVA Pl. 75, I and Pl. 76, I.
58. For the development and relationships between representations of the frontal quadriga in *Flachenkunst* and *Rundplastik*, G. Hafner, *Viergespanne in Vorderansicht*, 1938, 56 ff.
59. Reconstructions of the pediments are illustrated in John Boardman, José Dörig, Werner Fuchs, Max Hirmer, *L'Art Grec*, 1966, 109, figs. 157/158.
60. Cf. the Late Corinthian I olpe, Louvre E 648, with Laoptolemos in chariot, frontal-faced (Illus. 90), Edmond Pottier, *Vases antiques du Louvre*, Paris, 1897, 1, Pl. 51; Payne, 165 (nr. 39), 326 (nr. 1412). Cf. in Chalcidian ware, Cab. Méd. 202, neckamphora, Rumpf nr. 3, Pll. 7 ff. The frontal face is employed more freely in Chalcidian ware than in any other fabric and iconographic patterns and restraints noted in the present work do not apply here; in addition to depicting the frontal face proportionately more often than other vase painters, the Chalcidian artists employ it uniquely in relation to new types, e.g., the the frontal-faced equestrian, Louvre E 794, neck-amphora, Rumpf nr. 33, Pl. 67. For a frontal-faced helmeted warrior lying in a way uncharacteristic in Attic vase painting (but similar to the frontal-faced giant stretched out on his side from the Siphnian Treasury, cf. n. 33), see Taranto 65, amphora, Rumpf nr. 108, Pll. 114 f.

surrounding the tondo of a cup in the Vatican by Douris, a series of men and youths stand in what appears to be casual conversation; two of the youths' faces are frontal (FF 245-246, Illus. 93). Again, in a procession of pairs of men and youths, on a cup in the Louvre by the Triptolemos Painter, a bearded figure is shown with face frontal (Illus. 94). As the Early Classical period approached, groupings of figures tended to become more decorous and less energized than earlier in the Archaic period, in keeping with the sobriety that characterizes much art of the Early Classical period. Seen in this light, several neutral frontal faces can be understood as a partial solution to the formal problem of maintaining visual interest within the new and sober expressive mode. However, as one observes late Archaic scenes such as the conversation scene by Douris and the procession by the Triptolemos Painter, the explanation of formal variance seems insufficient. The independence from the profile convention conveys more than rhythmic variety. In these examples of heads that turn in our direction, we are witnessing within the context of vase painting an expression of the personal freedom which is a new keynote of the period. The new independence both from the dominant profile convention, and from the conventions that had governed and restricted representations of the frontal face as well are expressions of the sense of human freedom that the sculptors of this period learned to convey through the relaxation of the old symmetrical mode, and the invention of the ponderated pose.

In addition to the new uses of frontality, the weakening of the profile convention can be seen in another new development: the oblique view of the face is invented in the Late Archaic period.[61] The first indications of this development are small deviations in strictly frontal heads. While the hair and beard around the frontal face are usually rendered with an improbable symmetry, even in examples that are quite late (see the drinker by the Dokimasia Painter, Illus. 26), on a few black-figure examples, the beard may swing asymmetrically around a tilted face, as on the satyr on an amphora in the Vatican of the Leagros Group (FF 62). On the red-figure cup by the Kleophrades Painter in Bologna, the strands of Skiron's hair and beard swing down (Illus. 34); looking at Skiron on the cup by Douris in Berlin (Illus. 31), one could not guess Skiron's toppled position from the symmetry of his beard, but gravity pulls on the curly locks falling downward over his left shoulder.

Another deviation from simple facial frontality that occurs in the later Archaic vases is in the eyes, which may swing inward in collapse (Illus. 44) or in humourous concentration (Illus. 62), or upward in loss of control (Illus. 34). On the fragmentary skyphos in Florence (Illus. 54), the Kleophrades Painter has wittily relied on the unexpected asymmetry of the centaur's eyes pulled to the right by the power of lust, while the face remains frontal; even the hair seems drawn toward Iris, as if by a magnet. In some works of the Late Archaic period, one senses the artist's pull toward the oblique in the way the essentially frontal head is set on the neck of intrinsically dynamic figures, as in Onesimo's youth with a sponge in the Louvre (Illus. 47), or his athletes on the cup in Munich (Illus. 45).

The first truly oblique views identified lie in the purview of Douris and are datable to *ca.* 490. On the lekythos in the Cleveland Museum of Art attributed

---

61. A talk by the author, ''The Three-Quarter View Face: Origins, Development and Meanings,'' was presented at the *XIIè Congrès International d'Archéologie Classique,* to be published in the forthcoming congress *Proceedings.*

to Douris (Illus. 95), Enkelados falls before Athena who is represented on the other side of the vase.[62] The nose of the giant is seen almost directly from the front. However, the unsymmetrical facial contour, and the placement and rendering of features within it, remove this representation from frontality. The outer (open) corner of the eye on the right is nearer to the right edge of the face than is the outer (closed) corner of the eye on the left. The upper lip remains almost centered, as if locked in with the centered nose, but the lower lip is moved toward the right, yielding to the oblique conception. As Ariel Kozloff noted, this vase features a unique profile gorgoneion on the aegis of Athena; it is as though the artist expressed with it his awareness that he was experimenting with unconventional views of the face. On a fragmentary cup in the Cabinet des Médailles, Paris,[63] Douris represented the head of Ajax obliquely viewed and facing toward the left as the hero, like a grape-burdened satyr, carries the heavy body of Achilles. In this drawing, the oblique representation is slightly more advanced than that of Enkelados on the Cleveland vase in that the head is turned farther to the side, and the open corner of the far eye is coterminous with the facial contour. As in the Cleveland lekythos, the multiple points of view with which elements of the eyes, nose and mouth are represented, as well as a sketchy doubling of some contour lines, permit us to recognize the artist feeling his way toward oblique representation. These multiple points of view and sketchy contours demon-

---

62. Arielle P. Kozloff, The Art Institute of Chicago, *Greek Vase-Painting in Midwestern Collections*, W.G. Moon with L. Berge, 186 f., Pl. VI; the attribution is questioned by G.F. Pinney, *AJA* 85, Oct. 1981, 504. See also Boardman ARV, fig. on p. 138.
63. Paris, Bibliothèque Nationale, Cabinet des Médailles, 537 and 598, cup, frr. *ARV² 429, 19.*

strate the experimental status of these two drawings; through them, we are offered a glimpse into the artistic struggle to discover how the oblique view of the human face could be represented on a two-dimensional surface, a struggle which, once resolved, made it so easy to achieve for all artists of the western tradition who followed.

While these are the oblique views that can be plausibly dated to around 490 B.C., three-quarter views lose their rarity when one considers paintings that can in conventional terms be placed *ca.* 480, such as Procrustes falling before Theseus on the Kleophrades Painter's late stamnos in London, E 441, or the centaur victim on a cup in Munich, 2650, by the Foundry Painter.[64] It is interesting to observe the way the rare three-quarter views of approximately 490 B.C. increase greatly in relative frequency approximately ten years later.

Like the use of the frontal face for new types of figures, the invention of the oblique view can be described as a weakening of Archaic conventions. However, in this "weakening" can be seen artistic strength, for in it we can recognize the extension of inherited iconography to carry new ideas. These departures from iconographic patterns set down in the Archaic period convey a new definition of the human being. This release from the power of artistic convention is a visual metaphor of new spiritual insight, an expression of the growing spirit of individuation that marks the emerging Classical human image.

In reviewing the material, several specific reasons for frontal faces have been considered. During a period in which the exploration of new possibilities was a sig-

64. Kleophrades Painter stamnos, London, British Museum, E 441, Boardman ARV, fig. 137; Foundry Painter cup, Munich, Museum antiker Kleinkunst, 2640, Boardman ARV, fig. 268.

nificant artistic thrust, the use of the frontal face expanded the expressive range; thus, the smile, the grimace, the mouth open in song, in agony, in slackness, or even in vomiting, the eyes rolled up in joyous release, anguish, or vagueness and dislocation, or to the side in lust or wariness, the forehead furrowed in pain, all were given vivid graphic renderings through its use. The tilt of the tipsy satyr's head expresses the disequilibrium of intoxication. In formal terms, the frontal face was exploited in some cases for the rhythmic variety, as in the Affecter's use of frontality to energize his personal stylistic decorum, and, perhaps, in the use of frontality to vary the relatively static composition of some Late Archaic to Early Classical groupings. I have also suggested that, as a deviation from the stylistic convention, the frontal face in the Late Archaic period was used as a metaphor of individuation.

At the same time that we can appreciate the special possibilities offered by the frontal face, we can also identify the continuing constraint governing its use, seen in the narrow selectivity of figures who could be represented with faces frontal as well as in its rarity. Victims of combat and of athletic contest, and satyrs, komasts and symposiasts could be represented frontally, but beyond these there are very few frontal faces that are not related to one of these two major groupings. With few exceptions, gods are not shown with their faces frontal. Satyrs may be represented with frontal face but not maenads, losing warriors but not victors, Skiron and Kerkyon but not Theseus, Alkyoneus, Kyknos or Antaios but (with two exceptions) not Herakles, Enkelados but not Athena, Achilles dead, but not Achilles alive and fighting. Furthermore, one must bear in mind the numerous mythological, legendary, and genre subjects that are treated with absolutely no recourse to the frontal face. And for every one of the types that can be represented with frontal face, in the vast majority of cases, the depiction is in profile.

Part of the special treatment given the frontal face lies in properties intrinsic to its representation, particularly the kinetic power of the line of sight. As the most casual visitors to a museum have noted, the eyes in a head represented frontally seem to look at us directly, to meet our eyes, and even to follow us from side to side. Noting this phenomenon Schapiro describes the frontal figure as seeming "to exist both for us and for itself in a space virtually continuous with our own."[65] These elements of continuity between the world of the viewer and the world of the work of art, and of direct communication were antagonistic to important formal aims of Archaic vase painting. Martin Robertson's analysis of the surface aesthetic is significant in this connection; he writes that "The Greek vase decorator was always extremely conscious of the curved *surface* of the vase as his decorative field"; however, adherence to the curved surface picture plane was not absolute and thus the development of Archaic vase painting was punctuated by a series of "brilliant compromises between the emulation of free painting and the demands of decoration."[66] Three-dimensional subjects such as a ship with billowing sails, or a frontal quadriga, could be manipulated so as not to rupture the picture plane,[67] their appeal lying in the tension between their unmistakable three-dimensionality and their containment within the two-dimensional design. However, while such aggressively three-

65. *Op. cit.*, 39.
66. "The Place of Vase-painting in Greek Art," BSA 46, 1951, 154 f.
67. John White, *Perspective in Ancient Drawing,* London, 1956, 20 ff. on sails, shields and quadriga.

dimensional objects as the ship with billowing sails, or a frontal quadriga, could be tamed by design, the frontal human face, with its direct confrontation of the viewer, its insistent connection between the picture and the world, represented an intractable challenge, which helps to account for the rarity of its representation. Often as we have seen, frontal-faced figures actually seek our involvement, but even when they do not, we cannot avoid them.

However, these observations do not account for the *selective* rarity of the frontal face, the face that with almost no exceptions, examples of them fall within one of the two main groupings. Here, analysis indicates two fundamental factors governing the use of the frontal face: its position as a formal analogue for a state of diminished control, and the underlying presence of an iconographic model. In the broadest sense, for most of the Archaic period, the occasional frontal face punctuating the seemingly endless profile series, always slightly shocking, serves as a kind of reminder of the outer edges of experience where the idea of the willed intelligent act loses significance, and nature takes controlling hold. Recognition of this connotation helps to explain why Dionysos, whom one might expect to be regularly depicted with frontal face because of his association with masks and with drinking, is not so represented, there being only two exceptions among a multitude of pictures of him; this is too indecorous, too insecure a mode for a divinity, even for the god of wine. The present study also brings forth the importance of an iconographical model for the Attic vase painter. Although on the surface the two major groups of frontal faces appear unconnected, as we have seen an iconographical model links them, the Gorgon, connected with the satyr-group through the image of the mask, and with the victim-group through the representation of defeat. It is fair to say that behind almost

every frontal face in Attic vase painting of the Archaic
period lies, ultimately, the frontal face of the Gorgon.
The rarity of incidence has required the method of
collection of examples and analysis for the motif to be
better understood. For the present writer, even though
the collection of examples was undertaken with some
expectation of finding iconographical patterns that
might be governing the incidence of the frontal face,
an unexpected result that emerged from the study of
examples is the near omnipresence of iconographic
influence, and the tenacity of its hold. Even toward the
end of the Archaic period, when we see some of the
finest vase painters of the time extending the frontal
face to new figure types, and suggesting through it new
meanings, we can recognize that their inventions are
founded upon the creative transformation of the living
iconographical tradition.

LIST OF FRONTAL FACES

SATYRS

Black-Figure

1. *Satyr "Terpekelos" squats, with satyrs* (on back of handle). New York, Metropolitan Museum, 26.49, aryballos (spherical), from Attica. ABV 83,4, 682; Para. 30; BA 8: Nearchos. Boardman ABV, fig. 50. *Ca. 560. Illus. 74.*

2. *Satyr in Return of Hephaistos.* Oxford, Ashmolean Museum, 1920.107, amphora of Panathenaic shape. ABV 89,2 below; Para. 33; BA 9: the Burgon Group. *Ca. 560. Illus. 2.*

3. *Satyr in Return of Hephaistos.* Paris, Louvre, E 860, neck-amphora. ABV 103,111; BA 11: the Tyrrhenian Group. *Ca. 560-550.*

4. *Satyr in Return of Hephaistos.* Paris, Louvre, E 876, dinos. ABV 90,1; BA 9: the Painter of Louvre E 876. *Ca. 550.*

5. *Satyr in Return of Hephaistos* (arms raised). New York, Metropolitan Museum, 31.11.11, column-krater. ABV 108,5, 684; Para. 43; BA 12: Lydos. Boardman ABV, fig. 65; Michael A. Tiverios, *O Ludos kai to ergo tou,* 1976, Pll. 53-55; Schefold GHG, figs. 23-24. *Ca. 550. Illus. 4.*

6. *Satyr in Return of Hephaistos* (arms lowered). As nr. 5. The frontal face is largely lacking. *Illus. 5.*

7. *Satyr dances with satyrs and maenads.* Basle, Antikenmuseum, BS 424.1965, amphora. Tiverios, Pll. 96-97; CVA Basle 1, Pl. 28: "Dem Maler Lydos sehr nahe." *Ca. 550.*

8. *Satyr in Return of Hephaistos.* London, British Museum, 1914.3-17.6, cup. JHS 49, 1929, 269, nr. 52, Pl. XVI,9. *Ca. 550.*

9. *Satyr in Return of Hephaistos.* New York, Metropolitan Museum, 17.230.5, cup, from Vulci. Para. 78,1, above; BA 23: the Oakshott Painter. *550-540.*

10. *Satyr dances, with Dionysos and satyrs.* Naples, Museo Nazionale, 2725 (inv. 81178), amphora, from Etruria. ABV 133,6: Group E. *550-540.*

Satyrs: Black-Figure, continued

11. *Satyr dances, with Dionysos and satyrs.* Basle, Dr. Herbert Cahn, MMAG, and New York market, amphora. Para. 56, 27 *bis.*: Group E. André Emmerich Gallery, N.Y., *Art of the Ancients: Greeks, Etruscans and Romans,* 1968, nr. 7. 550-540.

12. *Satyr with Dionysos, satyrs and maenad.* Würzburg, Martin von Wagner-Museum, L 250, amphora. ABV 136,48: Group E. 550-540.

13. *Satyr dances, with Dionysos and satyrs.* Basle, Dr. Herbert Cahn, MMAG, amphora. MMAG, Auk.22, 1961, nr. 127: Group E. *Ca.* 540.

14. *Satyr dances, with Dionysos and satyrs.* Paris, Louvre F 55, amphora. ABV 133,4; Para. 55: Group E. *Ca.* 540-535.

15. *Satyr, with satyrs and maenad.* Budapest, Museum of Fine Arts, 50.189, amphora, from Vulci (?). Para. 61: Exekias. Dietrich von Bothmer, "An Amphora by Exekias," *Bulletin du Musée Hongrois des Beaux-Arts* 28, 1966, 17 ff.; cf. Mary B. Moore, "Horses by Exekias," *AJA* 72, 1968, 357 ff. 540-530. *Illus. 9-10.*

16. *Satyr with Dionysos, Hermes, male figure (Zeus?), satyr.* Boston, Museum of Fine Arts, 01.8053, amphora. ABV 246,72; BA 30: the Affecter. CVA Boston 1, Pl. 9, drawing 10; Heide Mommsen, *Der Affecter,* 1975, nr. 15, Pll. 2, 24, 138, Beil. N, Z. 550-540.

17. *Satyr with Dionysos, Hermes, female (Ariadne?), satyr.* As nr. 16. *Illus. 7.*

18. *Satyr with Dionysos, Hermes, female (Ariadne?), and satyr.* Baltimore, Walters Art Gallery, 48.11, amphora. ABV 245,69; BA 30: the Affecter. Mommsen, nr. 17, Pll. 2, 25, Beil. N. 550-540.

19. *Satyr with Dionysos, Ikarios (?), and male figure.* Vienna, Kunsthistorisches Museum, inv. IV 4399, amphora. Para. 111,68 *bis.;* BA 30: the Affecter. Mommsen, nr. 32, Pll. 3, 38. 540-530.

20. *Satyr with Dionysos and other figure.* Milan, Museo Archeologico Civico, 198, amphora, fr., from Chiusi. ABV 246,80; BA 31: the Affecter; joins Innsbruck, Universität-sammlung II, 12.13, fr.; Para. 111, 79 *bis.:* congruence noted by Bothmer. Mommsen, nrs. 60a (Milan) and 60 (Innsbruck), Pl. 70. 530-520. The frontal-faced satyr is on the Milan portion.

Satyrs: Black-Figure, continued

21. *Satyr dances (head partly interrupted by handle left of A), following maenad, with Dionysos and male figures.* Orvieto, Museo Civico, 1014, neck-amphora, from Orvieto. ABV 244,46; BA 29: the Affecter. Mommsen, nr. 92, Pll. 11, 100-101, Beil. K. *Ca.* 520. C. Kerényi, *Dionysos,* 1976, 147, suggests subject is Dionysos' arrival at the house of Semachos; Beazley (ABV 244) suggests arrival at house of Ikarios.

22. *Satyr dances, following maenad, hand to forehead* (under handle). As nr. 21.

23. *Satyr with Dionysos, Ariadne, satyr.* Orvieto, Museo Civico, 240, amphora, from Orvieto. ABV 246,73; BA 30: the Affecter. Mommsen, nr. 95, Pll. 12, 103-104, Beil. O, Z. *Ca.* 520.

24. *Satyr with Dionysos, Ariadne, satyr. As nr. 23.*

25. *Satyr with Dionysos, Ariadne, satyr.* As nr. 23. Nr. 23 on A, nrs. 24-25 on B.

26. *Satyr dances with maenad (under handle), with scenes of battle.* Orvieto, Museo Civico, 594, neck-amphora, from Orvieto. ABV 242,32; BA 29: the Affecter. Mommsen, nr. 96, Pll. 12, 105-106, Beil. I, Z. *Ca.* 520.

27. *Satyr dances, with Hermes, a goddess (?), and male figures.* Oxford, Ashmolean Museum, 1965.126, neck-amphora. ABV 242,34; Para. 110; BA 29: the Affecter. Boardman ABV, fig. 157; Mommsen, nr. 103, Pll. 13, 115, Beil. J. CVA Oxford 3, Pll. 4-5. *Ca.* 520.

28. *Satyr stoops beneath donkey in Return of Hephaistos.* Basle, Dr. Herbert Cahn, MMAG, neck-amphora. Para. 111,25 *ter.;* BA 29: the Affecter. MMAG, Auk. 34, 1967, nr. 125; André Emmerich Gallery, N.Y., *Art of the Ancients,* 1968, nr. 8. Mommsen, nr. 110, Pll. 14, 125, Beil. J. *Ca.* 520.

29. *Satyr with Dionysos, satyrs and youthful Hephaistos.* Florence, Museo Archeologico Etrusco, 3809, hydria. CVA Florence, Museo Nazionale V, III, H, Pll. 9, 3-4, 11,1-2. Cf. Frank Brommer, "Die Rückfuhrung des Hephaistos," JdI 52, 1937, 198 ff., esp. 202, 206. *Ca.* 540. *Illus. 3.*

30. *Satyr with satyrs, chasing woman (Hera?)* (on shoulder). Oxford, Ashmolean Museum, 1934.353, lekythos, fragmentary, from Greece. ABV 70,8; Para. 28: the Sandal Painter. *Ca.* 540. Brommer, *Satyrspiele,*73, under nr. 31, for theme in relation to satyr play.

Satyrs: Black-Figure, continued

31. *Satyr dances, with Dionysos and satyr.* Würzburg, Martin von Wagner-Museum, L 249, amphora. ABV 296,10; Para. 128; BA 39: the Painter of Berlin 1686. *Ca.* 540.

32. *Satyr with krotala dances, with maenads and satyrs.* Munich, Museum antiker Kleinkunst, 1371, amphora, from Vulci. ABV 297,14: the Painter of Berlin 1686. *Ca.* 540.

33. *Satyr dances, holds phallus, with maenads.* Würzburg, Martin von Wagner-Museum, L 178, neck-amphora. Ernst Langlotz, *Griechische Vasen in Würzburg,* 1932, Pl. 38. *Ca.* 540.

34. *Satyr pours wine for Dionysos, with satyrs.* Würzburg, Martin von Wagner-Museum, L 265, amphora, from Vulci (?). ABV 151,22 and 687; Para. 63; BA 19: the Amasis Painter. Boardman ABV, fig. 88; cf. Simon GV, Pl. 68; Robertson, *History,* Pl. 41a. 535-530.

35. *Satyr behind donkey with youth (Iacchos), Dionysos, satyrs and maenads* (zone around tondo). London, British Museum, B 427, cup. CVA London, British Museum 2, III H E, Pl. 20, 2. *Ca.* 530.

36. *Satyr carries hydria, with satyr.* Paris, Louvre F 227, neck-amphora. ABV 309,86: the Swing Painter. *Ca.* 530.

37. *Satyr squats, waves* (between handles). Berlin, Staatliche Museen, DDR, F 1671, neck-amphora, from Tarquinia. ABV 226,2: the BMN Painter, Nikosthenic workshop. 530-520. *Illus. 75.*

38. *Satyr squats, holds phallus* (between handles). As nr. 37. *Illus. 76.*

39. *Satyr walks, plays auloi.* Paris, Cabinet des Médailles, 258, oinochoe (olpe), from Vulci. ABV 229,VIII; Para. 108: Nikosthenic workshop, VIII. 530-520. *Illus. 59.*

40. *Satyr sits, plays auloi* (between eyes). Munich, Museum antiker Kleinkunst, 2088, cup, from Vulci. ABV 232, where noted that Hansjörg Bloesch, *Formen Attischer Schalen,* 1940, 25, nr. 13, identified the foot profile as Nicosthenic; BA 27. JdI 93, 1978, figs. 17-18. *Ca.* 530. *Illus. 60.*

41. *Satyr sits, plays auloi.* As nr. 40. *Illus. 61.*

42. *Satyr stoops carrying wine skin* (on neck). Paris, Louvre, F 115, neck-amphora. ABV 319,4; Para. 140: the Class of Cabinet des Médailles 218. 530-520.

Satyrs: Black-Figure, continued

43. *Satyr carries wine skin, with Dionysos reclining, satyrs and maenad.* Paris, Louvre, F 305, column-krater. CVA Paris, Louvre 2, III H e, Pll. 3, 5, 8. 530-520.

44. *Satyr dances, with Dionysos and Hermes.* Munich, Museum antiker Kleinkunst, SL 458, neck-amphora. ABV 257, 259,18; Para. 114; BA 33: Manner of the Lysippides Painter, the Mastos Group. CVA München 7, Pll. 358,3, 359,1-2, Beil. E 6. 530-520.

45. *Satyr dances, with Dionysos, Ariadne and satyrs in vintage scene.* Boston, Museum of Fine Arts, 01.8052, neck-amphora. ABV 242,35, 259, 26; Para. 110, 114; BA 29: Manner of the Lysippides Painter, the Mastos Group (figure scenes); the Affecter (pattern work). CVA Boston 1, Pl. 24, drawing 22; Mommsen nr. 102, Pll. 13, 113-114, Beil. J. *Ca.* 520

46. *Satyr runs in vintage scene, with satyrs.* As nr. 45. The vintage scene on side B is continuous with the scene with Dionysos and Ariadne on side A. *Illus. 6.*

47. *Satyr carries basket to treading table in vintage scene, with satyrs.* As nr. 45. *Illus. 6.*

48. *Satyr swings on grapevine in vintage scene, with satyrs.* As nr. 45.

49. *Satyr chases (or dances with) maenad* (tondo). Paris, Louvre, F 130, cup. ABV 262,49: Manner of the Lysippides Painter. 530-520.

50. *Satyr, one of two reclining at foot of vine while two (with profile heads) climb for grapes.* Basle, Dr. Herbert Cahn, MMAG, neck-amphora. MMAG, Auk. 51, 1975, nr. 129: Manner of the Lysippides Painter, connected with the Mastos Group. *Ca.* 520.

51. *Satyr reclining at foot of vine.* As nr. 50. These are the only certain examples known to me of frontal-faced satyrs leaning on their elbows, in the symposiast posture, cf. Cahn, *ibid.*, 50f.

52. *Satyr squats, arms held over knees* (under handle, between masks of Dionysos and satyr). Munich, Museum antiker Kleinkunst, N.I. 8518 (formerly 1480A), neck-amphora. ABV 275,4, 691; Para. 121; BA 36: Class of neck-amphorae with masks. CVA München 8, Pll. 380,1, 381, 382, 1-2, Beil. B 6.: the Long-Nose Painter. 530-520.

Satyrs: Black-Figure, continued

53. *Satyr squats, one hand over belly, other away from body.* As nr. 52.

54. *Satyr squats, head to left* (under handle). San Simeon, California, Hearst Collection, 5516 (=SSW 9848) neck-amphora. Para. 145: may be by the Long-Nose Painter. Evelyn E. Bell, *The Attic Black-Figure Vases at the Hearst Monument, San Simeon*, Diss. Univ. California, Berkeley, 1977, Pll. 13-14. 530-520. *Illus. 77.*

55. *Satyr squats, head to right* (under handle). As nr. 54. *Illus. 78.*

56. *Satyr stoops carrying wine skin* (under handle). London, British Museum, B 264, neck-amphora, from Vulci. ABV 288,19; BA 37: the Group of Würzburg 199, the Circle of the Antimenes Painter X. Mommsen, Pl. 134. 525-520.

57. *Satyr stoops carrying wine skin in Return of Hephaistos.* Once Durand, 126, cup. ABV 207,1: the Durand Painter. *Ca.* 520.

58. *Satyr bent over, grasping vines* (between eyes). Boston, Museum of Fine Arts, 03.784, cup. CVA Boston 2, Pl. 100, 1-4. *Ca.* 520.

59. *Satyr, with Dionysos, satyr and maenads.* Madrid, Museo Arqueológico Nacional, 11008, amphora (bilingual), from Vulci. ABV 294,24; Para. 128; BA 72: Psiax. Boardman ARV, fig. 14; Beth Cohen, *Attic Bilingual Vases and their Painters*, 1978, Pll. 63-64. Cf. ARV² 7,2 and 618; Para. 321. *Ca.* 520.

60. *Satyr dances, with maenads and satyr* (on shoulder). Munich, Museum antiker Kleinkunst, 1713, hydria. Eduard Gerhard, *Auserlesene Vasenbilder*, ii, 1843, Pl. 142. 520-510.

61. *Satyr carries Dionysos on his back.* Rome, Musei del Vaticano, 437, oinochoe, from Vulci. ABV 429,8 (below): the Class of Vatican G. 47 (Guide-Line Class merged with Class of Vatican G. 47, Para. 184). *Ca.* 510.

62. *Satyr dances, supported by satyr, with Dionysos, satyrs and maenads.* Rome, Musei del Vaticano, 371, amphora, from Vulci. ABV 367,91: the Leagros Group, the Antiope Group I. 510-500.

63. *Satyr seizes maenad, with Dionysos, satyr and maenad.* Rome, Museo Nazionale di Villa Giulia, 50619, neck-amphora. ABV 374,193: the Leagros Group. 510-500.

64. *Satyr behind horses of Dionysos' chariot, waves, in vintage and procession scene.* Paris, Cabinet des Médailles, 320, cup. ABV

Satyrs: Black-Figure, continued

389, where compared with a fragment close to the Chiusi Painter; BA 49. 510-500.

65. *Satyr with satyr and deer, flanking bird on tree.* Lecce, Museo Provinciale, 560, skyphos. C.H.E. Haspels, *Attic Black-Figured Lekythoi,* 1936, 250,34: the Theseus Painter; Para. 255. Cf. Michael M. Eisman, "The Theseus Painter, the Marathon Tumulus and Chronology," AJA 75, April 1971, 200. 505-495.

66. *Satyr with satyr and deer, flanking bird on tree.* As nr.65.

67. *Satyr with Herakles and Athena.* Basle, Mrs. Helen Kambli, skyphos, frr. Haspels 250,11: the Theseus Painter. Not seen by author; Haspels, 143, indicates that the satyr has a frontal face. 505-490?

68. *Satyr dancing, with Herakles enthroned and Athena.* London, British Museum, 1902.12-18.3, skyphos. Haspels, 249,9: the Theseus Painter. JHS 31,1911, fig. 4 on p. 4, fig. 5, p. 6. 505-495.

69. *Satyr, with Dionysos on donkey and satyrs.* London, British Museum, B 513, oinochoe. Haspels, 252,69: the Theseus Painter. 500-490.

70. *Satyr squats* (between eyes). Copenhagen, National Museum, 10702, cup, fr., from Orvieto. CVA Copenhagen, Musée National 8, III H, Pl. 327,3. 490-480. *Illus. 79.*

71. *Satyr leans on staff, with satyrs torturing woman.* Athens 1129, lekythos, from Eretria. Haspels, 266,1: the Beldam Painter, Pll. 49, 50,2, 51,1, p. 170. ABV 709, Para. 292. Boardman ABV, fig. 277. *Ca.* 480 or after.

Satyrs: Red-Figure

72. *Satyr kneels before seated Dionysos.* Boston, Museum of Fine Arts, 03.790, neck-amphora. ARV² 11,2: "shape and pattern-work somewhat recall the Three-Line Group." *Ca.* 525.

73. *Satyr seizes maenad.* London, British Museum, E 812.I and Cambridge, Fitzwilliam Museum, N.142, cup, frr. from Naucratis. ARV² 68,10: near Oltos. *Ca.* 520. The satyr, frontal face largely lost, is on the London portion.

Satyrs: Red-Figure, continued

74. *Satyr embraces maenad, with Dionysos, satyr and maenad.* Tarquinia, Museo Nazionale, RC 6843, amphora, from Tarquinia. ARV² 23,2, 1620; Para. 323; BA 74: Phintias. Charbonneaux *et al.*, fig. 380. AA 1983, fig. 8 on p. 476. 520-510. *Illus. 21.*

75. *Satyr seizes maenad* (tondo). Tarquinia, Museo Nazionale, RC 2066, cup, from Tarquinia. ARV² 126,23, 1627; BA 87: the Nikosthenes Painter. Potter signature: Pamphaios. 520-510.

76. *Satyr holds (ejaculates into?) neck-amphora* (tondo). Kassel, Staatliche Kunstsammlungen, AL 5204, cup. Potter signature: Pamphaios. AA 1983, figs. 1-2 on p. 472, with attribution (open to question) to the Nikosthenes Painter by Peter J. Connor; P. Gercke, *Funde aus der Antike Sammlung Paul Dierichs,* 1981, 111 ff. 520-510.

77. *Satyr lugs pointed amphora* (tondo). Munich, Museum antiker Kleinkunst, 2613, cup, from Vulci. ARV² 136,3, 1628; Para. 334: the Poseidon Painter. *Ca.* 515.

78. *Satyr, "Satyros," carries pointed amphora, with Dionysos on donkey, satyrs and maenad.* Würzburg, Martin von Wagner-Museum, H 1646 (474), cup, from Vulci. ARV² 173,10; BA 92: the Ambrosios Painter. *Ca.* 510.

79. *Satyr holds skyphos, with satyr carrying wineskin on his back.* Geneva, market, Koutoulakis, cup. Conrad, Pl. 11,1, after Bothmer photo collection. *Ca.* 510.

80. *Satyr with satyrs, maenads and donkeys.* Laon, Musée Archéologique Municipal, 37.1054, cup, from Vulci. ARV² 150,23, 1628: Manner of the Epeleios Painter. 510-500. *Illus. 12-13.*

81. *Satyr carries volute-krater in Return of Hephaistos.* Cambridge, Mass., Harvard University, Fogg Art Museum, 1960.236, calyx-krater. ARV² 185,31; BA 93: the Kleophrades Painter. *The Frederick M. Watkins Collection, Fogg Art Museum, Harvard University, 1973,* nr. 20. *Ca.* 500.

82. *Satyr, with satyrs robbing Herakles* (on shoulder). Salerno, Museo Civico, 1371, hydria. ARV² 188,67; Para. 341; BA 94: the Kleophrades Painter. Greifenhagen, *Neue Fragmente des Kleophradesmalers,* 1972, Pl. 26,2. Brommer, *Satyrspiele,* 76, nr. 76, for relation to satyr play. *Ca.* 500.

Satyrs: Red-Figure, continued

83. *Satyr plays auloi, with maenads, satyrs and Dionysos.* Munich, Museum antiker Kleinkunst, 8732 (2344), pointed amphora, from Vulci. ARV² 182,6, 1632; Para. 340; BA 93: the Kleophrades Painter. Charbonneaux *et al.*, figs. 387-388; Boardman ARV, fig. 132; Simon GV, Pll. 120-124, XXXIII-XXXIV; cf. Greifenhagen, *Neue Fragmente*, Pl. 32 and fig. 2. 500-490. *Illus. 62.*

84. *Satyr plays auloi, with Dionysos.* Paris, Louvre, G 196, amphora. ARV² 296,2: the Troilos Painter. *Ca.* 490. *Illus. 63.*

85. *Satyr somersaulting, with satyrs dancing, riding phallus-bird, and somersaulting.* Brussels, Musées Royaux d'Art et d'Histoire, A 723, cup. ARV² 317, 15: the Proto-Panaetian Group (ii). *Ca.* 500.

86. *Satyr dancing, with satyrs and maenads.* Munich, Museum antiker Kleinkunst, 2638, cup, from Cervetri. ARV² 456,1, 1654: the Magnoncourt Painter. 500-490.

87. *Satyr holds thyrsus, with satyrs and maenads.* Paris, Louvre, G 34, cup. ARV² 456, where resemblance to the Magnoncourt Painter noted. 500-490.

88. *Satyr with ithyphallic donkey.* Orvieto, Museo Faina, 54, cup. Conrad, pl. 10,5, after Bothmer photo collection. *Ca.* 490.

89. *Satyr, with ithyphallic donkey.* As nr. 88.

90. *Satyr, squeezes self under arms of maenad mounting chariot, and satyrs.* Athens, Acropolis, 787, column-krater, frr., from Athens. ARV² 233,1 above: the Group of Acropolis 787. 490-480.

91. *Satyr kneels over krater in front of altar of Dionysos, waves, with satyr.* Paris, Louvre, G 227, pelike. ARV² 283,2 below: the Painter of Louvre G 238. *Ca.* 480.

92. *Satyr scans distance while attacking a sleeping maenad, with satyr and sleeping maenad.* Once Goluchow, Museum Czartoryski, 119, rhyton (ram's head). ARV² 382,185, 1649; Para. 366; BA 113: the Brygos Painter. Boardman ARV, fig. 257. 480-470. For date cf. Herbert Hoffman, "The Persian Origin of the Attic Rhyta," AntK 4, 1961, 21. *Illus. 8.*

93. *Satyr: "head-frontal-, shoulders, breast, of a satyr to right, bending."* Philadelphia, market, cup, fr. ARV² 1651: recalls the Foundry Painter. Not seen by author; Beazley indicates head frontal. 490-470?

Satyrs: Red-Figure, continued

94. *Satyr dances, with maenads and satyrs.* Boston, Museum of Fine Arts, 00.499, cup, from Orvieto. ARV² 435,89; Para. 375; BA 117: Douris. 490-480. Cf. Diana M. Buitron, *Douris,* Diss., Institute of Fine Arts, New York, 1976, 210, chronology.

95. *Satyr dances, with Dionysos, maenads and satyrs.* Cambridge, Mass., Harvard University, Fogg Art Museum, 1925.30.129, cup, from Capua. ARV² 436,112; BA 117: Douris. 490-480. *Illus. 23.*

96. *Satyr dances, with Dionysos, maenads and satyrs.* Munich, Museum antiker Kleinkunst, 2647, cup, from Vulci. ARV² 438,132, 1653: Douris. 480-470.

97. *Satyr carries pointed amphora, with satyrs, in scene in which large satyr threatens smaller one.* Rome, Musei del Vaticano, 16541 (569), cup, from Vulci. ARV² 451,1, 1653, 1654; Para. 376; BA 119: the Oedipus Painter, Manner of Douris III. Boardman ARV, fig. 301. 480-470. The frontal-faced satyr is retained on the Etruscan imitation of this cup, Musée Rodin,980, N. Plaoutine, JHS 57, 1937, 22 ff.; Beazley, *Etruscan Vase-Painting,* 1947, 25 ff.; cf. Brommer, *Satyr-spiele,* 80 f., nr. 157, fig. 34 and p. 40.

98. *Satyr dances, holds drinking horn.* Once Goluchow, Museum Czartoryski, 1226, cup. CVA Cracovie, fascicule unique, III I c, Pl. 8, 2. *Ca.* 480 (or after).

KOMASTS, SYMPOSIASTS

Black-Figure

99. *Komast, with komasts, dances.* Kassel, Staatliche Kunstsammlungen, T 386, neck-amphora, from Cervetri. ABV 99,61, 684; BA 11: the Tyrrhenian Group; Para. 35 and 38: the Castellani Painter. CVA Kassel 2, Pll. 17, 18,2. 570-560.

100. *Komast, with komasts, dances.* Paris, Louvre, E 832, neck-amphora. ABV 100, 74: the Tyrrhenian Group. *Ca.* 570-550.

101. *Komast, with women and komasts.* Copenhagen, National Museum, Chr. VIII 323, neck-amphora, from Vulci. ABV 102,97, 684: the Tyrrhenian Group; Para. 38: the Prometheus Painter. 560-550. *Illus. 14.*

Komasts, Symposiasts: Black-Figure, continued

102. *Komast, with women and komasts.* As nr. 101. *Illus. 15.*

103. *Komast, with komasts and women, dances.* Munich, Museum antiker Kleinkunst, 1431, neck-amphora, from Vulci. ABV 102,99; BA 11: the Tyrrhenian Group. CVA München 7, Pll. 315,3, 316,1, 317, Beil. A4. 560-550. *Illus. 16.*

104. *Komast, with women and komasts, dances.* Palazzolo Acreide, cup, from Akrai. ABV 34,1: the Palazzolo Painter, Komast Group: VII. *Ca.* 560.

105. *Komast, with woman, dances.* Cambridge, Mass., Harvard University, Fogg Art Museum, 1925.30.13, cup. ABV 34,2 (below): the Palazzolo Painter, Komast Group: VII. *Ca.* 560.

106. *Komast, with women and komasts, dances.* Göttingen, Universität, J. 11, cup. ABV 35,4 above: the Palazzolo Painter, Komast Group: VII. *Ca.* 560.

107. *Symposiast.* As nr. 4. *Illus. 17.*

108. *Komast dances, with komasts.* Stuttgart, Museum, Kas. 76, lekythos. CVA Stuttgart 1, Pl. 19, 3-4: related to Haspels' Blackneck Class. 550-540.

109. *Komast.* Munich, Museum antiker Kleinkunst, A 895, hydria. Gaston Vorberg, *Die Erotik in der Antike in Kleinkunst und Keramik,* 1921, Pl. 70. 550-540.

Komasts, Symposiasts: Red-Figure

110. *Komast plays auloi.* Rome, Musei del Vaticano, 17752 (G 71), hydria (kalpis), from Vulci. ARV² 28,14; BA 75: Euthymides. Boardman ARV, fig. 35. 520-510. *Illus. 64.*

111. *Symposiast "Thodemos" with symposiasts and player of auloi.* Munich, Museum antiker Kleinkunst, 8935, calyx-krater, frr. ARV² 1619, 1705; Para. 322,3 *bis.;* BA 73: Euphronios. E. Vermeule, AntK 8, 1965, 34 ff., Pll. 11, 12,1, 13,1; only the top of Thodemos' head was known at this time and its frontality was not apparent; MüJb: 17, 1967, 245 ff.; 22, 1971, 229 ff.; 24, 1973, 241; 26, 1975, 214 f; Boardman ARV, fig. 25; Bothmer, AA 1976, 503 ff., figs. 24-26. *Ca.* 510. *Illus. 18.*

112. *Hetaira reclining with cup to lips, with hetairai.* Leningrad, Hermitage Museum, B. 1650 (644), psykter, from Cervetri. ARV² 16,15; Para. 509; BA 73: Euphronios. Boardman ARV, fig. 27. 510-500. *Illus. 19.*

Komasts, Symposiasts: Red Figure, continued

113. *Komast (or satyr?) in or behind large vessel* (tondo). Sidney, Cambitoglou, cup, fr. ARV² 84, 18 *ter.:* Skythes. *Ca.* 510.

114. *Komast, embraces woman.* Paris, Louvre, G 13, cup. ARV² 86, alpha; BA 84: the Pedieus Painter. Boardman ARV, fig. 92; CVA Paris, Louvre 19, I b, Pll. 68, 1-2, 69, 1-3, fig. on p. 45. *Ca.* 510. *Illus. 22.*

115. *Symposiast with cup to lips.* Gotha, Museum, 48, cup (white ground), from Kolias. ARV² 20, where Beazley comments on influence of artists like Euphronios and the Sosias Painter; Para. 322; BA 74. Boardman ARV, fig. 51; Joan Mertens, *Attic White-Ground,* 1977, Pl. 26,3. 510-500.

116. *Symposiast (or satyr), reclining.* Oxford, Ashmolean Museum, 1929.165, plate, fr. ARV² 78,101: Epiktetos. 510-500. Beazley identified the figure as a satyr; although the hair is long, there are no specific satyr attributes visible, and the motif of the figure reclining on a cushion suggest that a symposiast may be represented; cf. FF 51.

117. *Symposiast "Kleonumos".* Rome, Museo Nazionale di Villa Giulia, cup, from Cervetri. ARV² 173,5, Para. 338: the Ambrosios Painter. 510-500.

118. *Youth "Ermodoros" plays auloi at symposium.* As nr. 117.

119. *Symposiast, plays kottabos.* Florence, Museo Archeologico, PD 248, cup, from Orvieto. ARV² 121,1: Near Apollodoros. *Ca.* 500.

120. *Komast, male love-making.* Turin, Museo di Antichità, 4117 (Coll. Canino nr. 3032), cup. ARV² 150, 35: Manner of the Epeleios Painter; ARV² 1628, withdrawn from list. CVA Torino (III) III I, Pll. 3,1-2, 4,1-2. *Ca.* 500. A scene similarly obscene, with a different arrangement of figures, also with a frontal-faced man, occurs on a pinax, Athens, National Museum, Acropolis, 1040, *ca.* 500, Boardman ARV, fig. 18.

121. *Symposiast with cup to lips.* London, market, Christie's, once Northampton, Castle Ashby, cup, from Vulci. ARV² 455,8; BA 119: the Ashby Painter. CVA Castle Ashby, nr. 58. Pll. 36, 62. *ca.* 500.

122. *Symposiast plays auloi.* London, British Museum, E 64, cup, from Vulci. ARV² 455,9, 1654; BA 119: the Ashby Painter. AntK 11, Pl. 24, 2-4. *Ca.* 500. *Illus. 65.*

Komasts, Symposiasts: Red-Figure, continued

123. *Symposiast with cup to lips.* Basle, Dr. Herbert Cahn, 116 (ex Rome, de Ferrari) cup. ARV² 316,3, 1645: the Proto-Panaetian Group (i); BA 106. Cf. Dyfri Williams, *Jb. der Berliner Museen* 18, 1976, figs. 11-14, for attribution of "early Onesimos." *Ca.* 500.

124. *Komast grasped around waist by komast, with komast and women.* Leningrad, Hermitage Museum, 651, cup, from Capua. ARV² 325,77; Para. 511: Onesimos. *Ca.* 490.

125. *Komast with cup, dances.* Boston, Museum of Fine Arts, 98.930, cup. ARV² 431,45; Para. 374: Douris. 495-490. *Illus. 24.*

126. *Komast with cup, dances, waves?* (hand near forehead). London, British Museum, E 53, cup, from Vulci. ARV² 435, 87: Douris. 490-480.

127. *Youth supporting drunken man.* Karlsruhe, Badishes Landesmuseum, 70.395, cup. Jürgen Thimme, Ernst Petrasch, *Bildhefte des Badischen Landesmuseums Karlsruhe, Griechische Vasen,* 1975, Pll. 37-39: Douris (Cahn, Wegner, Metzler); attribution not accepted by Bothmer. *Ca.* 480.

128. *Symposiast with cup to lips.* As nr. 127. Nr. 127 on A, nr. 128 on B.

129. *Youth (Oinopion?) pours wine for Dionysos.* Paris, Louvre, G 138, cup. ARV² 365,61; BA 110: the Triptolemos Painter. 490-480. *Illus. 94.*

130. *Symposiast with cup to lips.* Berlin, Staatliche Museen, F 2298, cup, from Vulci. ARV² 364,52; Para. 364; BA 110: the Triptolemos Painter. Boardman ARV, fig. 305. *Ca.* 480.

131. *Komast (or satyr) dancing, and boy (?).* Florence 10 B 180, cup. ARV² 335,9: the Antiphon Painter. *Ca.* 480. *Illus. 67.*

132. *Symposiast plays kottabos.* Göttingen, Universität, J.32, cup. ARV² 344,47: Manner of the Antiphon Painter. *Ca.* 480.

133. *Symposiast with skyphos to lips.* Paris, Louvre, G 133, cup. ARV² 348, 7: the Cage Painter, Related to the Antiphon Group, I. *Ca.* 480.

134. *Symposiast plays auloi.* Leipsig, Karl-Marx-Universität, T 3367, cup. ARV² 467,122; BA 120: Makron. *Ca.* 480. *Illus. 66.*

Komasts, Symposiasts: Red-Figure, continued

135. *Symposiast (head tied with red fillet)*.Athens, Acropolis, 477, skyphos, fr., from Athens, Acropolis. Botho Graef and Ernst Langlotz, *Die antiken Vasen von der Akropolis zu Athen, 2,* 1933, Pl. 38. *Ca.* 480.

136. *Symposiast, vomiting, head held by youth.* Copenhagen, National Museum, 3880, cup, from Italy. ARV² 373,36, 1649: "Close to the Brygos Painter but might be by the Dokimasia Painter"; Para. 366, 372,11 *ter.:* the Dokimasia Painter, "Mild Brygan;" BA 112. CVA Copenhagen, Musée National 3, III, I, Pll. 141-142. *Ca.* 480. *Illus. 26.*

137. *Komast holds skyphos, dances.* As nr. 136. Nr. 136 in tondo, nr. 137 on exterior.

138. *Symposiast plays kottabos.* Boston, Museum of Fine Arts, 01.8034, cup. ARV² 401,11 f.; Para. 370: the Foundry Painter. *Ca.* 480.

139. *Komast holds skyphos, dances.* Toledo, Ohio, Museum of Art, 64.126, cup. Para. 370,12 *bis.;* BA 114: the Foundry Painter. CVA Toledo 1, Pll. 55-56, figs. 10-12; Warren G. Moon with Louise Berge, *Greek Vase Painting in Midwestern Collections,* The Art Institute of Chicago, 1980, nr. 101. *Ca.* 480.

140. *Komast with staff (dances?).* Philadelphia, University Museum, 2445, cup, from Vulci. ARV² 420,60: the Painter of the Paris Gigantomachy, Circle of the Brygos Painter IV. *Ca.* 480.

141. *Komast with staff, dances.* As nr. 140. Nr. 140 in tondo, nr. 141 on exterior.

142. *Komast, "Anacreontic".* Brussels, Musées Royaux d'Art et d'Histoire, R 332, cup. ARV² 380,169: the Brygos Painter. 480-470. For Beazley's Anacreontic series, L.D. Caskey, J.D. Beazley, *Attic Vase Paintings in the Museum of Fine Arts, Boston,* ii, 1954, 58 ff., this nr. 11.

143. *Symposiast with cup.* Bayonne, Musée Bonnat, 217, rhyton (ram's head). Probably 480-470 (cf. FF 92).

COMBAT FIGURES

Black-Figure

144. *Eurytion fallen between Herakles and Geryon.* London, British Museum, B 194, amphora, from Vulci. ABV 136,56; Para. 55: Group E. 540-535. *Illus. 27.*

Combat Figures: Black-Figure, continued

145. *Warrior fallen between two warriors.* Brussels, Musées Royaux d'Art et d'Histoire, R 318, neck-amphora. ABV 308,72: the Swing Painter. *Ca. 530. Illus. 28.*

146. *Eurytion fallen between Herakles and Geryon.* As nr. 42. Nr. 42 on neck, nr. 146 on body.

147. *Warrior fallen before a quadriga.* Munich, Museum antiker Kleinkunst, 1563, neck-amphora. CVA München 8, Pll. 363,2, 365, 367,2, Beil. A 2, where related to the Lysippides Painter. *Ca. 520. Illus. 29.*

148. *Warrior fallen between Achilles and Memnon, with Eos and Thetis (?).* Brussels, Musées Royaux d'Art et d'Histoire, A 712, neck-amphora. ABV 320,3, 693; BA 41: the Three-Line Group. Boardman ABV, fig. 217. 520-510.

149. *Enkelados felled by Athena.* Tours, Musée des Beaux-Arts, 863.2.66, neck-amphora. CVA Tours fascicule unique, III H e, Pl. 8, where related to the Group of the Small Neck-amphorae, near the Red-Line Painter. 520-510.

150. *Geryon slain by Herakles.* Delos, Museum, 547, lekythos, from Delos. ABV 379,274; Para. 163, 167-168: the Leagros Group, the Class of Delos 547. 515-500.

151. *Kyknos, defeated by Herakles.* Worcester, Mass. Art Museum, Austin S. Garver Fund 1966.63, neck-amphora. Buitron, *Attic Vase Painting in New England Collections,* Fogg Art Museum, Harvard University, 1972, nr. 19: the Leagros Group (Bothmer). 515-500. For the subject, H.A. Shapiro, ''Herakles and Kyknos,'' AJA 88, Oct. 1984, 523 ff., this vase Pl. 68,4.

152. *Alkyoneus sleeping, about to be slain by Herakles.* Toledo, Ohio, Museum of Art, 1952.66, lekythos. Andreae, JdI 77, 1962, 170 where attributed to the Leagros Group. CVA Toledo 1, Pll. 27, 3-4, 28,1. 510-500.

153. *Achilles, borne by Ajax.* Munich, Museum antiker Klein-kunst, 1415, amphora. CVA München 1, Pll. 2, 46,2, 47,3, 52,6 where related to the Leagros Group. *Ca. 510. Illus. 32.*

154. *Alkyoneus (?) sleeping, about to be slain by Herakles.* Civitavecchia, Museo Civico (missing), and Munich, private collection, hydria, frr. ABV 332,22; Para. 146; BA 44: the Priam Painter. *Ca. 510.* The sleeping man with frontal face is on the Munich portion. Schefold GHG, 141 f., fig. 187.

Combat Figures: Black-Figure, continued

155. *Antaios in combat with Herakles, with Athena.* Athens, Market, skyphos. Haspels, 250,18: the Theseus Painter. 505-495? Not seen by author; Haspels, 143, indicates the face of Antaios is frontal.

156. *Polyphemus attacked by Odysseus and his men.* Berlin, Staatliche Museen, 3283, skyphos. Haspels 253,16: near the Theseus Painter. ABV 704; Para. 259; BA 62. 505-495. For the relation between Polyphemus and Alkyoneus compositions, see Berthold Fellman, *Die antiken Darstellungen des Polyphemabenteuers*, 1972, 28 ff., fig. 11.

157. *Hector dragged behind Achilles' chariot.* Paris, Cabinet des Médailles, lekythos. Haspels, 226,13: the Sappho Painter. Hildegund Gropengiesser, *Tainia, Festschrift für Rolande Hampe zum 70. Geburstag,* I, 1980, 317 and n. 44, fig. 5. 500-480.

158. *Kyknos defeated by Herakles.* Heidelberg, Universität, L 29, lekythos. ABV 574,2 (middle, above); Para. 289; BA 65: the Group of Athens 14645, near the Haimon Group (ii). CVA Heidelberg 4, Pl. 173, 1-3. *Ca.* 480.

159. *Alkyoneus sleeping, about to be slain by Herakles.* Athens, National Museum, 16350, lekythos. ABV 587, 1, above; Para. 292; BA 66: the Beldam Painter. *Ca.* 480 or after.

Combat Figures: Red-Figure

160. *Warrior falling* (between eyes). Cleveland, Museum of Art, 76.89, cup. ARV^2 7,7; Para. 321; BA 72: Psiax; ARV^2 38,8: Eye-cups A. iv, the Group of Leipsic T 3599. Schefold *Wort und Bild,* Pl. 4, 3-4; Boardman ARV, fig. 15; *Cleveland Museum of Art Bulletin* 64, 1977, fig.; Schefold GHG, fig. 311 (Hector?); Cohen, Pl. 57, 1-2; AntK 22, 1979, Pl. 13, 1,2,4,6; Moon with Berge, nr. 60. 520-510.

161. *Herakles wrestling with Nereus, lifting him from ground.* Rome, Museo Nazionale di Villa Giulia, cup, from Cervetri. ARV^2 1623, 66 *bis.;* Para. 327; BA 81: Oltos. Charbonneaux *et al.,* fig. 362. *Ca.* 510. *Illus. 35.*

162. *Kyknos slain by Herakles.* Dallas, Hunt Collection, calyx-krater. M. Robertson, "Euphronios at the Getty," *J. Paul Getty Museum Journal* 9, 1981, 29 ff., figs. 13-18: Euphronios. *Wealth of the Ancient World,* Fort Worth, 1983, no. 6. 510-500.

Combat Figures: Red-Figure, continued

163. *Youth bent to knee grasping hero around waist, separating fighting heroes.* Leiden, Rijksmuseum van Oudheden, PC 85 (xviii h 36), amphora, from Vulci. ARV² 32,1, below; BA 75: the Pezzino Group. CVA Leiden 3, Pll. 116, 117, 118, 1-3, 119, 1-3, fig. 8. 510-500.

164. *Warrior fallen before assailant.* London, British Museum, E 43, cup. ARV² 118,13, 1627; BA 86: the Epidromos Painter. Boardman ARV, fig. 114. 510-500.

165. *Alkyoneus sleeping, about to be slain by Herakles.* Melbourne, National Gallery of Victoria, 1730.4, cup, from Vulci. ARV² 125,20; Para. 333; BA 87: the Nikosthenes Painter; potter signature: Pamphaios. Charbonneaux *et al.*, fig. 368; Boardman ARV, fig. 95. AA 1983, fig. 7 on p. 475. 510-500. *Illus. 33.*

166. *Warrior fallen between two warriors.* Cambridge, Fitzwilliam Museum, GR.19.1937, cup. ARV² 135,13: wider circle of the Nikosthenes Painter; resemblance to Bonn Painter noted. 510-500. *Illus. 50.*

167. *Alkyoneus sleeping, about to be slain by Herakles.* Switzerland, private collection, cup. JdI 77, 1962, Pll. 1-14, where attributed to "the Alkyoneus Painter." 510-500.

168. *Warrior fallen in Iliupersis.* Athens, Acropolis, A190, cup, fragmentary, from the Acropolis. Graef and Langlotz 2, Pl. 10, nr. 212. BCH 54, 1930, 448, nr. 20; *Hesperia* 5, 1936, 257 f., fig. 5; AJA 58, 1954, Pl. 62, fig. 28. *Ca.* 500.

169. *Herakles robbed by satyrs* (on shoulder). As nr. 82. Herakles is a comic victim in this scene, rather than a tragic figure like other frontal-faced victims.

170. *Skiron thrown by Theseus.* Paris, Cabinet des Médailles, 536 (part), 647, part of 535, and other frr., cup, from Tarquinia. ARV² 191,104; BA 94: the Kleophrades Painter. Of the face, only part of Skiron's beard is preserved. 500-490.

171. *Astyanax, dead, lying across lap of Priam in Iliupersis (Death of Priam).* Naples, Museo Nazionale, 2422, hydria (kalpis), from Nola. ARV² 189,74, 1632; Para. 341; BA 94: the Kleophrades Painter. Charbonneaux *et al.*, fig. 386; Boardman ARV, fig. 135; Simon GV, Pll. 128-129; Robertson *History*, Pl. 80. 480-475. *Illus. 36.*

Combat Figures: Red-Figure, continued

172. *Skiron thrown by Theseus.* Bologna, Museo Civico, PU 270, cup, probably from Chiusi or vicinity. ARV² 192,107, 1632: the Kleophrades Painter. 480-475. *Illus. 34.*

173. *Astyanax held upside-down (by the legs) by Neoptolemos in Iliupersis (Death of Priam).* Berlin, Staatliche Museen, F 2281 (missing), and Rome, Musei del Vaticano, also probably Berlin F 2280, frr., cup. ARV² 19,1, 19, 2; BA 74: Manner of Euphronios. D. Williams, *Jb. der Berliner Museen* 18, 1976, 9 ff., attributes to early Onesimos. *Ca. 500.*

174. *Warrior dead in Iliupersis (Death of Priam).* (?) As nr. 173.

175. *Alkyoneus sleeping, about to be slain by Herakles.* Cambridge, Mass., Emily Dickinson Blake Vermeule Collection, cup, frr. Buitron, *Attic Vase Painting in New England Collections,* nr. 49, where noted it is related to the Proto-Panaetian Group by von Bothmer. Williams, *ibid.,* attributes to early Onesimos. *Ca. 490.*

176. *Kerkyon in headlock by Theseus.* Paris, Louvre, G 104 and Florence, Museo Archeologico, PD 321, cup, from Cervetri. ARV² 318,1, 1645; Para. 358; BA 106: Onesimos. *Ca. 490.*

177. *Troilos attacked in front of altar by Achilles.* Perugia, Museo Civico, 89, cup, from Vulci. ARV² 320,8; Para. 359; BA 107: Onesimos. 490-480. *Illus. 37.*

178. *Giant fallen before Dionysos.* Berlin, Staatliche Museen, F 2321, kyathos, from Vulci. ARV² 333,3: the Oinophile Painter, Manner of Onesimos (ii). *Ca. 490.*

179. *Skiron thrown by Theseus.* London, British Museum, E 48, cup, from Vulci. ARV² 431,47, 1653; BA 117: Douris. 490-480.

180. *Warrior (Persian) fallen before Greek opponent.* Paris, Louvre, G 117, cup. ARV² 433,62; Para. 375; BA 117: Douris. 490-480.

181. *Warrior fallen before opponent.* Berlin, Staatliche Museen, F 2287, from Cervetri, Leipsig, Karl-Marx-Universität, fr., Tübingen, Universität, E 21, fr., cup. ARV² 433,68-70, 1653; Para. 375: Douris. 490-480. *Illus. 44.*

182. *Skiron thrown by Theseus.* Paris, Louvre, G 126 plus fr., cup. ARV² 438,129, 1706; Para. 375: Douris. 480-470.

183. *Skiron thrown by Theseus.* Berlin, Staatliche Museen, F 2288, cup, from Vulci. ARV² 438,130, 1701; BA 117: Douris. 480-470. *Illus. 31.*

Combat Figures: Red-Figure, continued

184. *Warrior fallen between two warriors.* As nr. 183. Nr. 183 in tondo, nr. 184 on exterior. *Illus. 30.*

185. *Warrior fallen to his knee.* Rome, Museo Nazionale di Villa Giulia, 50318, cup. ARV² 158: may be by the Painter of Berlin 2268. AA 1927, 166, fig. 27. 500-480.

186. *Warrior attacked by two others.* Leipsig, Karl-Marx-Universität, T 513, cup, from Orvieto. ARV² 364,43: the Triptolemos Painter. *Ca.* 490.

187. *Aigisthus slain by Orestes as Clytaemnestra flees.* Basle, Dr. Herbert Cahn, 42, stamnos, fragmentary. ARV² 1648, 6 *bis.;* Para. 364; BA 110: the Triptolemos Painter. *Ca.* 480.

188. *Troilos, fallen from horse, attacked by Achilles.* Palermo, Museo Nazionale, V 659, cup, from Chiusi. ARV² 480,2, below: Makron. *Ca.* 490. *Illus. 38.*

189. *Warrior, probably a Trojan, fourth of six running with warriors, with Ajax and Achilles playing a board game.* Florence, Museo Nazionale, 3929, cup. ARV² 460,15 (see also 433,64); BA 120: Makron. 490-480.

190. *Troilos on horseback, grabbed by hair by Achilles.* Paris, Louvre, G 154, cup. ARV² 369,3; BA 111: the Brygos Painter. 490-480. *Illus. 39.*

191. *Warrior fallen between Achilles and Memnon, with Eos and Thetis.* Tarquinia, Museo Nazionale, RC 6846, cup, from Tarquinia. ARV² 369,4, 406; Para. 365; BA 111: the Brygos Painter. 490-480. *Illus. 25.*

192. *Orpheus attacked by Thracian women.* Zurich, Universität, 3477 (ex Philadelphia market), stamnos. ARV² 1652; Para. 373, 34 *bis.;* BA 115: the Dokimasia Painter, "Mild Brygan". Boardman ARV, fig. 277; JdI 95, 1980, fig. 6. *Ca.* 470.

193. *Argus felled by Hermes.* Paris, Louvre, G 229, pelike, from Vulci. ARV² 289,3, 1642: the Siren Painter; ARV² 254,4: the Class of Cabinet des Médailles 390. *Ca.* 480.

194. *Enkelados felled by Athena.* London, British Museum, E 165, hydria, from Vulci. ARV² 294,62, BA 105: the Tyszkiewicz Painter. Boardman ARV, fig. 187. 480-470.

PALAESTRA FIGURES

Black-Figure

195. *Wrestler, lifted from ground.* Munich, Museum antiker Kleinkunst, 1461, amphora of Panathenaic shape. *Ca. 525. Illus. 40.*

196. *Wrestler, at disadvantage.* Rome, Musei del Vaticano, 34584 (414), stamnos, from Vulci. ABV 343,3, below; BA 45: the Michigan Painter, the Perizoma Group I. *Ca. 515.* Cf. Barbara Philippaki, *The Attic Stamnos,* 1967, 12 f. *Illus. 41.*

Red-Figure

197. *Wrestler, lifted from the ground.* Berlin F 2159, amphora, from Vulci. ARV² 3,1, 1671; Para. 320; BA 71: the Andokides Painter. Charbonneaux *et al.*, fig. 342; Simon GV, Pll. 81-85; Boardman ARV, fig. 3. *Ca. 525. Illus. 42.*

198. *Boxer felled by boxer.* London, British Museum, E 39, cup, from Vulci. ARV² 430,29, 1653; BA 116: Douris. 495-490. *Illus. 43.*

199. *Wrestler engages opponent.* Munich, Museum antiker Kleinkunst, 2637, cup, from Vulci. ARV² 322,28, 1645; Para. 359; BA 107: Onesimos. Boardman ARV, fig. 227. *Ca. 490. Illus. 45.*

200. *Jumper with halteres.* As nr. 199. *Illus. 45.*

201. *Acontist standing.* As nr. 199. *Illus. 45.*

202. *Boxer wields blow.* Boston, Museum of Fine Arts, 1972.44 (ex Swiss, Private) cup. ARV² 322.37: Onesimos. *Illus. 46.*

203. *Youth washing with a sponge* (tondo). Paris, Louvre, G 291, cup. ARV² 322,36, 1706: Onesimos. *Ca. 480. Illus. 47.*

204. *Wrestler engages opponent.* Leningrad, Hermitage Museum, 656, cup. ARV² 331,17; Para. 511: Manner of Onesimos (i). 485-480.

205. *Wrestler (pankration) in body hold, about to be reprimanded for unfair play.* London, British Museum, E 78, cup, from Vulci. ARV² 401,3, 1651; Para. 370; BA 114: the Foundry Painter. Boardman ARV, fig. 263. *Ca. 480.* Gardiner explains the action, JHS 26, 1906, 6, fig. 1.

206. *Youth with himation in palaestra scene holds stick to mark start or finish line.* Philadelphia, University Museum, 4872, stamnos, from Orvieto. ARV² 215,11, 1635; Para. 345: Manner of the Berlin Painter (i). 480-470.

CENTAURS

Black-Figure

207. *Centaur holds stones, with centaurs armed with stones.* Paris, Louvre, E 849, neck-amphora. ABV 98,41: the Tyrrhenian Group. 570-560. *Illus. 51.*

208. *Centaur in Centauromachy* (on shoulder). Athens, Agora Museum, P 13126, amphora, fragmentary, from Athens, Agora. AA 1938, 56, fig. 9. *Hesperia* 8, 1939,232 f., fig. 30; *Hesperia* 15, 1946, 126, nr. 8, Pll. XVII,5 and XVIII. *Ca.* 560. *Illus. 52.*

209. *Centaur, holds stones* (tondo). Rome, Musei del Vaticano, Astarita 492, cup (bilingual). ARV² 44,81, 55,22; BA 77 and 80: Oltos. Cohen, Pl. 87, 2-3. *Ca.* 515-510.

Red-Figure

210. *Centaur with branch and rock* (tondo). Karlsruhe, Badisches Landesmuseum, 63.104, cup. ARV² 1700, 12 *ter.*, Para. 323; BA 74: Phintias. Thimme *et al.*, Pll. 24-26; Boardman ARV, fig. 39; Simon GV. Pl. 98. 520-510. *Illus. 53.*

211. *Centaur seizes Iris.* Florence, Museo Nazionale, 4218, skyphos, fragmentary. ARV² 191,102; BA 94: the Kleophrades Painter. Boardman ARV, fig. 139. *Ca.* 480. See Brommer, *Satyrspiele*, 73 f. on relation to satyr play. *Illus. 54.*

MAENADS

Black-Figure

212. *Maenad, dancing, with Dionysos, maenad and satyr.* Cracow, University, inv. 302, cup. ABV 640,103: the Leafless Group. 480-470.

Red-Figure

213. *Maenad dances, with maenads, Dionysos and satyr.* Basle, Mrs. Arthur Wilhelm, hydria (kalpis), from Vulci. ARV² 189,73, 1632; Para. 341; BA 94: the Kleophrades Painter. AntK 1, 1958, Pll. 2-4, 5,7-8; Boardman ARV, fig. 136. *Ca.* 480.

214. *Maenad carried off by two satyrs.* Rome, market, Basseggio, cup. ARV² 404,2: Manner of the Foundry Painter. Conrad, Pl. 16,3, after Bothmer photo collection. *Ca.* 480

MUSES

Black-Figure

215. *Muse (one of Nysai), plays syrinx in Wedding of Peleus and Thetis.* Athens, Acropolis, 587, dinos, frr., from Athens. ABV 39,15, 681; BA 4: Sophilos. Boardman ABV, fig. 25; Guven Bakir, *Sophilos*, 1981, Pll. 3-5. 580-570.

216. *Muse plays syrinx in Wedding of Peleus and Thetis.* London, British Museum, 1971.11-1.1, dinos. Para. 19,16 *bis.;* BA 4: Sophilos. A. Birchall, *The British Museum Quarterly* 36, 3-4, 1972, Pll. 34-37. Boardman ABV, fig. 24; Robertson *History*, Pl. 35a. Bakir, Pll. 1-2. 580-570. *Illus. 57.*

217. *Muse, Kalliope, plays syrinx in Wedding of Peleus and Thetis.* Florence, Museo Archeologico, 4209, volute-krater, from Chiusi. ABV 76,1, 682; Para. 29 f.; BA 7 f.: Kleitias. Charbonneaux *et al.*, figs. 64-69; Boardman ABV, fig. 46; Simon GV, Pll. 51-57, figs. 1-3; Robertson *History*, Pll. 35b, 37a. 570-565. *Illus. 56.*

NEREID

Red-Figure

218. *Nereid flees as Peleus seizes Thetis.* Munich, Museum antiker Kleinkunst, 8738, stamnos. ARV^2 209,161, 1633; Para. 343; BA 97: the Berlin Painter. AntK 14, 1971, Pl. 21,2. *Ca.* 480. *Illus. 69.*

DEITIES AND A TITAN

Black-Figure

219. *Dionysos in Wedding of Peleus and Thetis.* As nr. 217. *Illus. 56.*

220. *Dionysos seated between eyes.* Boulogne, Musée Communal, 559, cup. Cf. K. Schauenburg in *Studien zur griechischen Vasenmalerei*, AntK Suppl. 7, Pl. 16,1. *Illus. 58.*

221. *Athena, in Birth of Athena.* Richmond, Virginia, Museum of Fine Arts, 60.23, amphora, Para. 56,48 *ter.;* BA 16: Group E. Schefold GHG, fig. 5. 550-540. *Illus. 84.*

222. *Zeus, in Birth of Athena.* As nr. 221. *Illus. 84.*

223. *Prometheus with the daughters of Okeanos.* Munich, Museum antiker Kleinkunst, 1540, neck-amphora. CVA München 8, Pll. 428,2, 429, 430,5, Beil. F. 10, where related to the Kleophrades Painter. Schefold GHG, fig. 57. 510-500. *Illus. 86.*

Deities: Red-Figure, continued

224. *Nike flying, holds thymiaterion.* Paris, Louvre, G 199, neck-amphora, part, fr. ARV² 199,35, cf. 36; BA 95: the Berlin Painter. AntK 14, 1971, Pl. 8,4. *Ca.* 490. *Illus. 70.*

225. *Nike flying over altar, holds thymiaterion and phiale.* London, British Museum, E 513, oinochoe. ARV² 210,184; Para. 345; BA 97: the Berlin Painter. AntK 14, 1971, Pl. 8,3. *Ca.* 490. *Illus. 71.*

226. *Nike flying.* Palermo, Museo Nazionale, V 670, lekythos, from Selinus. ARV² 211,195; Para. 343: the Berlin Painter. 490-485. *Illus. 72.*

227. *Nike flying, holds oinochoe and cup.* Basle, Dr. Herbert Cahn, MMAG, lekythos. AntK 14, 1971, p. I (advertisement page); MMAG *Sonderliste N,* 1971, nr. 17: the Berlin Painter. 480-470.

FEMALE, MISC.

Red-Figure

228. *Woman lying down, with man, in scene of lovemaking.* New York, Metropolitan Museum, 19.182.32, cup, fr., from Cervetri. ARV² 231,80: the Eucharides Painter. *Ca.* 490. The woman's ear and part of a sakkos (?) remains. *Illus. 82.*

229. *Woman seated, resting head on pillow (feet on floor).* Athens, National Museum, 1584, tripod pyxis. ARV¹ 955: Manner of the Panaitios Painter. CVA Athens 1, III 1 c, Pl. 6,3. 490-480.

230. *Woman with arms upraised (Cassandra ?), in Homecoming of Paris.* As nr. 191. *Illus. 73.*

231. *Woman (hetaira ?) at her toilette, looks in mirror, holding alabastron, with wash tub and kalathos.* Paris, Louvre, G 282, S 1350, S 3916, and New York, Metropolitan Museum, 69, 44.2 a-d, also Louvre, C 11397 and Würzburg, Martin von Wagner-Museum, 484, frr., cup. ARV² 432, 60 f., 436,106, 437, 117, 1706: Douris. 490-480. For the kalathos, Gerhard Rodenwaldt, *Spinnende Hetären,* AA 1932, col. 7 ff.; cf. Eva C. Keuls, *The Reign of the Phallus,* 1985, pp. 252 ff. *Illus. 83.*

232. *Woman with fillet.* Providence, Rhode Island School of Design, 25.087, alabastron, from Greece. ARV² 363, 29 *bis.;* BA 110: the Triptolemos Painter. CVA Providence 1, Pl. 20,

Female, Misc.: Red-Figure, continued

2. 480-470. Bridget K. Hamanaka suggests that the woman is about to tie a fillet on a funerary monument, *Aspects of Ancient Greece, Allentown Art Museum,* 1979, 80 f. and figs. For the view that she is spinning, S.B. Luce, AJA 35, 1931, 300 f.

233. *Woman running in scene of Amymone pursued by Poseidon.* Taranto, Museo Nazionale and Reggio, Museo Nazionale, lekanis, from Locri. ARV² 212, 215 and 1634; BA 97: the Berlin Painter. 480-470. For subject, AntK 14, 1971, 54 and n. 64, Pl. 22.

MALE, MISC.

Black-Figure

234. *Man stung by bees.* London, British Museum, B 177, amphora. Para. 134 (under 21 *quater*). CVA London, British Museum 2, III H E, Pl. 32,1. 530-520. *Illus. 80.*

235. *Charioteer in frontal quadriga.* Basel, Dr. Herbert Cahn, MMAG Auk. 40, 1969, nr. 70. *Ca.* 520. For relationships of shape and ornament, *loc. cit.*

236. *Charioteer in frontal quadriga.* Toronto, Royal Ontario Museum, 926.19.2 (303), neck-amphora, from Vulci. ABV 272,100; BA 35: the Antimenes Painter. *Cleveland Museum of Art Bulletin* 66, Feb. 1979, fig. 3. *Ca.* 520. *Illus. 88.*

237. *Warrior in frontal quadriga, behind charioteer.* Cleveland, Museum of Art, 75.1, hydria. *Cleveland Museum of Art Bulletin* 66, Feb. 1979, figs. 1, 2,4: the Antimenes Painter. Moon with Berge, nr. 61. *Ca.* 520. *Illus. 89.*

238. *Warrior standing to right of quadriga.* As nr. 237. *Illus. 89.*

Red-Figure

239. *Youth standing, wearing himation.* Once Canino, neck-amphora (?), from Vulci. ARV² 184,21: the Kleophrades Painter. *Ca.* 500. Greifenhagen, *Neue Fragmente,* Fig. 3 on p. 43, after Eduard Gerhard, *Berlin Apparatus* XVI, 17.

240. *Youth standing, wearing himation, head tilted to side and held in hand, with youths.* As nrs. 82 and 169. Nrs. 82 and 169 on shoulder; nr. 240 on body. Greifenhagen interprets the subject as pairs of lovers, *Neue Fragmente,* 42, Pl. 26, 2. *Ca.* 500.

Male, Misc.: Red-Figure, continued

241. *Scythian resting.* Basle, Dr. Herbert Cahn, MMAG, cup. MMAG, *Sonderliste N*, 1971, nr. 74, where attributed to the Painter of the Agora Chairias Cup. *Ca.* 500.

242. *Youth holds hare.* As nr. 202; Nr. 242 is in tondo, nr. 202 is on exterior.

243. *Man leans on stick, dictating.* Oxford, Ashmolean Museum, G 138, 3,5,11, cup, frr. ARV² 326,93; Para. 359; BA 107: Onesimos. 490-480. *Illus. 91.*

244. *Youth leans against column in school scene.* As nr. 243. Nr. 243 is in tondo, nr. 244 on exterior. *Illus. 91.*

245. *Youth with men and youths.* Rome, Musei del Vaticano, 16545, cup, from Cervetri. ARV² 437,116, 1653; Para. 375: Douris. 490-480.

246. *Youth, with arm raised, with men and youths.* As nr. 245; both on exterior, opposite sides. *Illus. 93.*

247. *Man with men and youths (paired) in procession.* As nr. 129. Nr. 129 in tondo, nr. 247 in zone around tondo. 490-480. *Illus. 94.*

248. *Man listening at cithara contest.* Leningrad, Hermitage Museum, 614, pelike. ARV² 288,11; Para. 511; BA 104: the Argos Painter. *Ca.* 480.

249. *Bellows-pumper behind kiln in foundry.* Berlin, Staatliche Museen, F 2294, cup, from Vulci. ARV² 400, 1, 1651, 1706; Para. 370; BA 114: the Foundry Painter. Charbonneaux *et al.*, fig. 409; Simon GV, Pl. 158; Boardman ARV, fig. 262; *Hesperia* 46, 1977, Pl. 98; Robertson *History*, Pl. 59. *Ca.* 480. *Illus. 81.*

250. *Man, perhaps in procession.* Tübingen, Universität, E 26, cup, fr., ARV² 411,7: Manner of the Briseis Painter (i), "Mild Brygan". *Ca.* 480. For the symposiast fillet, see Caskey and Beazley, i, text, 28 f., and n. 1.

251. *Midas leading captured Silene.* Amsterdam, Allard Pierson Museum and Freiberg, University, (ex. Hauser), cup, frr. F. Brommer in *Studien zur griechischen Vasenmalerei*, AntK Suppl. 7, 1970, Pl. 30,3, after drawing by Hartwig, with bibliog. pp. 62 f. *Ca.* 480.

252. *Youth tunes lyre, seated next to standing man (teacher).* Paris, Louvre, G 333, lekythos. *Ca.* 480. *Illus. 92.*

253. *Old man seated, with youths.* Paris, Louvre, G 318, cup. ARV² 348,3; BA 109: the Cage Painter, related to the Antiphon Group I.

ADDENDUM

120A. *Symposiast.* Malibu, J. Paul Getty Museum, Acc. no. 76AE.132.1B, dinos, frr., red-figure. M. Robertson, "Fragments of a Dinos and a Cup Fragment by the Kleophrades Painter," *Greek Vases in the J. Paul Getty Museum*, I, 1983, fig. 4: the Kleophrades Painter. *Ca.* 500. The frontal face is largely lacking.

153A. *Alkyoneus about to be slain by Herakles.* Malibu, J. Paul Getty Museum, Acc. no. 81.AE.10.5, volute-krater, black-figure. F. Brommer, "Herakles und Theseus auf vasen in Malibu," *Greek Vases in the J. Paul Getty Museum*, II, 1985, fig. 1, where related to the Leagros Group. *Ca.* 510.

Nr. 152 is illustrated in *Greek Vases in the J. Paul Getty Museum*, II, 1985, figs. 25 a-b. Nr. 154 is illustrated with a drawing, *ibid.*, fig. 22. Nr. 216 is illustrated in *Greek Vases in the J. Paul Getty Museum*, I, 1983, figs. 1-13.

INDEX OF ARTISTIC REFERENCE:
ARTIST, GROUP AND CLASS NAMES

Names of artists, groups, classes	*Frontal Face numbers*
Acropolis 787, Group of	90.
Affecter	16, 17, 18, 19, 20, 21, 22, 23, 24, 25, 26, 27, 28, 45, 46, 47, 48.
Agora Chairias Cup, Painter of the	241.
"Alkyoneus Painter"	167.
Amasis Painter	34.
Ambrosios Painter	78, 117, 118.
Andokides Painter	197.
Antimenes Painter	236, 237, 238; Circle of the, 56.
Antiope Group	62.
Antiphon Group, related to the	133, 253.
Antiphon Painter	131; Manner of the, 132.
Apollodoros, near	119.
Argos Painter	248.
Ashby Painter	121, 122.
Athens 14645, Group of	158.
Beldam Painter	71, 159.
Berlin Painter	218, 224, 225, 226, 227, 233; Manner of the, 206.
Berlin 1686, Painter of	31, 32.
Berlin 2268, May be by the Painter of	185.
Blackneck Class, Related to the	108.
BMN Painter	37, 38.
Bonn Painter, resembles	166.
Briseis Painter, Manner of the	250.
Burgon Group	2.
Brygos Painter	92, 142, 190, 191, 230; Close to, 136, 137; Circle of, 136, 137, 140, 141, 192, 250.
Cabinet des Médailles 218, Class of	42, 146.
Cabinet des Médailles 390, Class of	193.
Cage Painter	133, 253.
Castellani Painter	99.
Chiusi Painter, comparison	64.
Delos 547, Class of	150.
Dokimasia Painter	136, 137, 192.

Names of artists, groups, classes	*Frontal Face numbers*
Douris	94, 95, 96, 125, 126, 127, 128, 179, 180, 181, 182, 183, 184, 198, 231, 245, 246; Manner of, 97.
Durand Painter	57.
Epeleios Painter, Manner of the	80, 120.
Epidromos Painter	164.
Epiktetos	116.
Eucharides Painter	228.
Euphronios	111, 112, 162; Manner of, 173, 174. Influence, 115.
Euthymides	110.
Exekias	15.
Foundry Painter	138, 139, 205, 249; Manner of, 214; Recalls, 93.
Group E	10, 11, 12, 13, 14, 144, 221, 222.
Guide-Line Class	61.
Haimon Group, Near the	158.
Kleitias	217, 219.
Kleophrades Painter	81, 82, 83, 120A, 169, 170, 171, 172, 211, 213, 239, 240; Related to, 223.
Komast Group	104, 105, 106.
Leafless Group	212.
Leagros Group	62, 63, 150, 151, 152; Related to, 153, 153A.
Leipsic T 3599, Group of	160.
Long-Nose Painter	52, 53; May be by, 54, 55.
Louvre E 876, Painter of	4, 107.
Louvre G 238, Painter of	91.
Lydos	5, 6; Near, 7.
Lysippides Painter, Manner of the	44, 45, 46, 47, 48, 49, 50, 51; Related to, 147.
Mastos Group	44, 45, 46, 47, 48; Connected with, 50, 51.
Magnoncourt Painter	86; Resembles, 87.
Makron	134, 188, 189.
Michigan Painter	196.
Nearchos	1.
Neck-amphorae with masks, Class of	52, 53.
Nikosthenes Painter	75, 76, 165; Wider Circle of, 166.
Nikosthenic Workshop	37, 38, 39, (40), (41).
Oakshott Painter	9.

Names of artists, groups, classes | *Frontal Face numbers*

Oedipus Painter — 97.

Oinophile Painter — 178.

Oltos — 161, 209; Near, 73.

Onesimos — 123, 124, 173, 174, 175, 176, 177, 199, 200, 201, 202, 203, 242, 243, 244; Manner of, 178, 204.

Palazzolo Painter — 104, 105, 106.

Pamphaios — 75, 76, 165.

Panaitios Painter, Manner of
  Cf., Proto-Panaetian Group — 229.

Paris Gigantomachy, Painter of the — 140, 141.

Pedieus Painter — 114.

Perizoma Group — 196.

Pezzino Group — 163.

Phintias — 74, 210.

Poseidon Painter — 77.

Priam Painter — 154.

Prometheus Painter — 101, 102.

Proto-Panaetian Group — 85, 123, 175.

Psiax — 59, 160.

Red-Line Painter, Near the — 149.

Sandal Painter — 30.

Sappho Painter — 157.

Siren Painter — 193.

Skythes — 113.

Small Neck-amphorae, Related to
  the Group of the — 149.

Sophilos — 215, 216.

Sosias Painter — Influence, 115.

Swing Painter — 36, 145.

Theseus Painter — 65, 66, 67, 68, 69, 155; near, 156.

Three-Line Group — 148; "Somewhat recall the," 72.

Triptolemos Painter — 129, 130, 186, 187, 232, 247.

Troilos Painter — 84.

Tyrrhenian Group — 3, 99, 100, 101, 102, 103, 207.

Tyszkiewicz Painter — 194.

Vatican G. 47, Class of — 61.

Würzburg 199, Group of — 56.

Without artistic reference — 8, 29, 33, 35, 43, 58, 60, 70, 79, 88, 89, 98, 109, 135, 143, 168, 195, 208, 220, 234, 235, 251, 252.

INDEX OF COLLECTIONS

Collection	Frontal Face numbers
Amsterdam, Allard Pierson Museum	251.
Athens, Agora Museum	208.
Athens, National Museum	71, 159, 229.
Athens, Acropolis Collection in the National Museum	90, 135, 168, 215.
Athens, Market	155.
Baltimore, Walters Art Gallery	18.
Basle, Antikenmuseum	7.
Basle, Dr. Herbert Cahn	123, 187.
Basle, Dr. Herbert Cahn, Münzen u. Medaillen AG	11, 13, 28, 50, 51, 227, 235, 241.
Basle, Mrs. Helen Kambli	67.
Basle, Mrs. Arthur Wilhelm	213.
Bayonne, Musée Bonnat	143.
Berlin, Staatliche Museen Preussischer Kulturbesitz	130, 156, 173, 174, 178, 181, 183, 184, 197, 249.
Berlin, Staatliche Museen zu Berlin, DDR	37, 38.
Bologna, Museo Civico	172.
Boulogne-sur-Mer, Musée Communal	220.
Boston, Museum of Fine Arts	16, 17, 45, 46, 47, 48, 58, 72, 94, 125, 138, 202, 242.
Brussels, Musées Royaux d'Art et d'Histoire	85, 142, 145, 148.
Budapest, Hungarian Museum of Fine Arts	15.
Cambridge, England, Fitzwilliam Museum	73, 166.
Cambridge, Massachusetts, Emily Dickinson Blake Vermeule Collection	175.
Cambridge, Massachusetts, Harvard University, Fogg Art Museum	81, 95, 105.
Canino, Lucien Bonaparte, Principe di, Collection	239.
Northampton, Castle Ashby	121.
Civitavecchia, Museo Civico	154.
Cleveland, Ohio, Museum of Art	160, 237, 238.
Copenhagen, National Museum	70, 101, 102, 136, 137.
Cracow, University	212.

Collection	*Frontal Face numbers*
Dallas, Texas, Hunt Collection	162.
Delos, Museum	150.
Durand Collection	57.
Florence, Museo Archeologico Etrusco	29, 119, 131, 176, 189, 211, 217, 219.
Freiburg, University	251.
Geneva, Market, Koutoulakis	79.
Goluchow, Museum Czartoryski	92, 98.
Gotha, Museum	115.
Göttingen, Universitätsammlung	106, 132.
Heidelberg, Universitätsammlung	158.
Innsbruck, Universitätsammlung	20.
Karlsruhe, Badisches Landesmuseum	127, 128, 210.
Kassel, Staatliche Kunstsammlungen	76, 99.
Laon, Musée Archéologique Municipal	80.
Lecce, Museo Provinciale Sigismondo Castromediano	65, 66.
Leiden, Rijksmuseum van Oudheden	163.
Leipsig, Karl-Marx-Universität	134, 181, 186.
Leningrad, Hermitage Museum	112, 124, 204, 248.
London, British Museum	8, 35, 56, 68, 69, 73, 122, 126, 144, 164, 179, 194, 198, 205, 216, 225, 234.
London, Market, Christie's	121.
Madrid, Museo Arqueológico Nacional	59.
Malibu, J. Paul Getty Museum	120A, 153A.
Melbourne, National Gallery of Victoria	165.
Milan, Museo Archeologico Civico	20.
Munich, Museum antiker Kleinkunst	32, 40, 41, 44, 52, 53, 60, 77, 83, 86, 96, 103, 109, 111, 147, 153, 195, 199, 200, 201, 218, 223.
Munich, private collection	154.
Naples, Museo Nazionale	10, 171.
New York, Metropolitan Museum of Art	1, 5, 6, 9, 228, 231.
Orvieto, Museo Civico	21, 22, 23, 24, 25, 26.
Orvieto, Museo Faina	88, 89.

Collection   *Frontal Face numbers*

Oxford, Ashmolean Museum   2, 27, 30, 116,
                                                                243, 244.

Palazzolo Acreide, Museo Judica   104.

Palermo, Museo Nazionale   188, 226.

Paris, Bibliothèque Nationale, Cabinet des Médailles   39, 64, 157, 170.

Paris, Musée du Louvre   3, 4, 14, 36, 42, 43,
                                                                49, 84, 87, 91, 100,
                                                                114, 129, 133, 146,
                                                                176, 180, 182, 190,
                                                                193, 203, 207, 224,
                                                                231, 247, 252, 253.

Perugia, Museo Civico   177.

Philadelphia, University (of Pennsylvania) Museum   140, 141, 206.

Philadelphia, Market   93, 192.

Providence, Rhode Island School of Design   232.

Reggio di Calabria, Museo Nazionale   233.

Richmond, Virginia, Museum of Fine Arts   221, 222.

Rome, Musei del Vaticano   61, 62, 97, 110, 173,
                                                                174, 196, 209,
                                                                245, 246.

Rome, Museo Nazionale di Villa Giulia   63, 117, 118, 161, 185.

Rome, Market, Basseggio   214.

Salerno, Museo Civico   82, 169, 240.

San Simeon, California, Hearst Foundation
    Collection   54, 55.

Sidney, Cambitoglou   113.

Stuttgart, Museum   108.

Switzerland, Private Collection   167, 202.

Taranto, Museo Nazionale   233.

Tarquinia, Museo Nazionale Tarquiniense   74, 75, 191, 230.

Toledo, Ohio, Museum of Art   139, 152.

Toronto, Royal Ontario Museum   236.

Tours, Musée des Beaux-Arts   149.

Tübingen, Universität   181, 250.

Turin, Museo di Antichità   120.

Vienna, Kunsthistorisches Museum   19.

Worcester, Massachusetts, Art Museum   151.

Würzburg, University, Martin von Wagner-Museum   12, 31, 33, 34, 78, 231.

Zurich, Universität   192.

FRONTAL FACES
IN ATTIC VASE PAINTING
OF THE ARCHAIC PERIOD

ILLUSTRATIONS

1. Paris, Musée du Louvre, E 874, dinos. The Gorgon Painter. H. with stand 93 cm. Photo: Chuzeville.

2. FF 2. Oxford, Ashmolean Museum, 1920.107, amphora of Panathenaic shape. The Burgon Group. H. 37 cm. Photo: Museum.

3. FF 29. Florence, Museo Archeologico, 3809, hydria. H. 36 cm. Photo: Soprintendenza alle Antichità, Firenze.

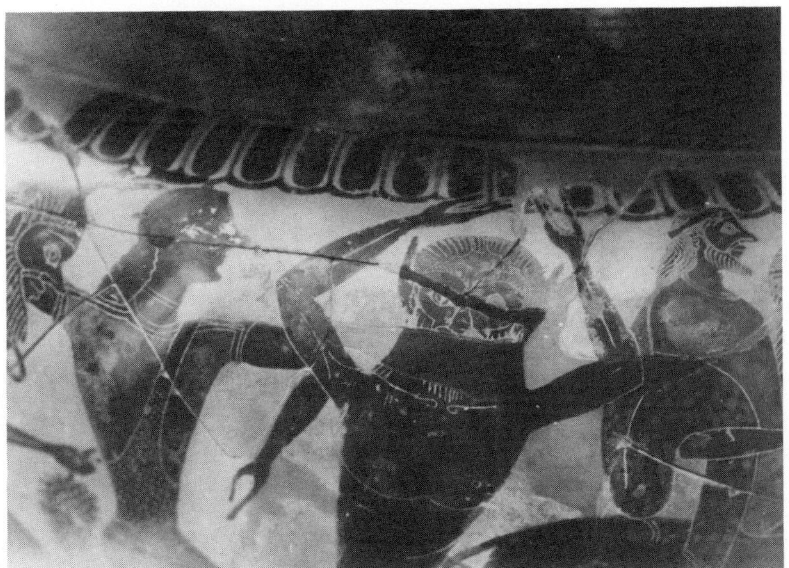

4. FF 5. New York, Metropolitan Museum of Art, 31.11.11, column-krater. Lydos. H. 56.5 cm. Photo: author.

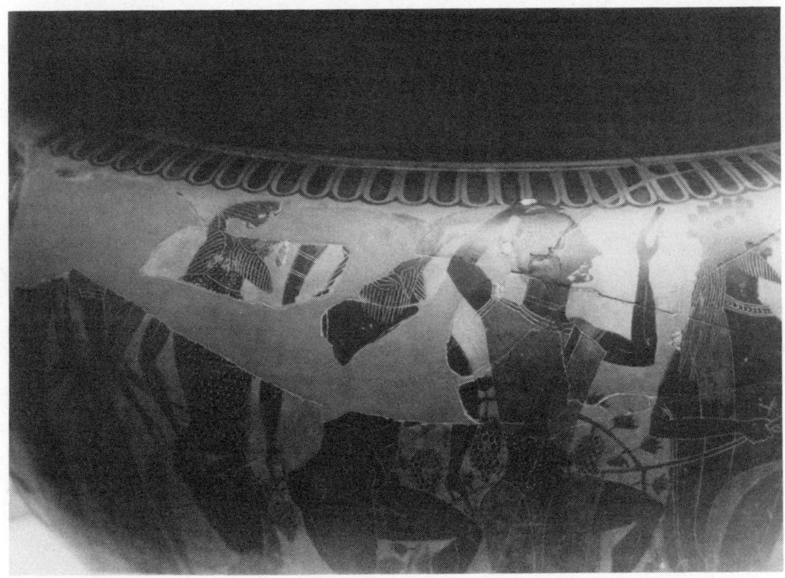

5. FF 6. As FF 5, illus. 4. Photo: author.

YVONNE KORSHAK

6. FF 46-47. Boston, Museum of Fine Arts, 01.8052, neck-amphora. Manner of the Lysippides Painter, (figures), the Affecter (pattern work). H. 42.9 cm. Photo: Museum, H.L. Pierce Fund.

7. FF 17. Boston, Museum of Fine Arts, 01.8053, amphora. The Affecter. H. 45.6 cm. Photo: Museum, H.L. Pierce Fund.

8. FF 92. Once Goluchow, Museum Czartoryski, 119, rhyton. The Brygos
Painter. H. 21 cm. Dm. mouth 11 cm. Photo after J.D. Beazley, *Greek Vases
in Poland*, 1928, Pl. 10, 4.

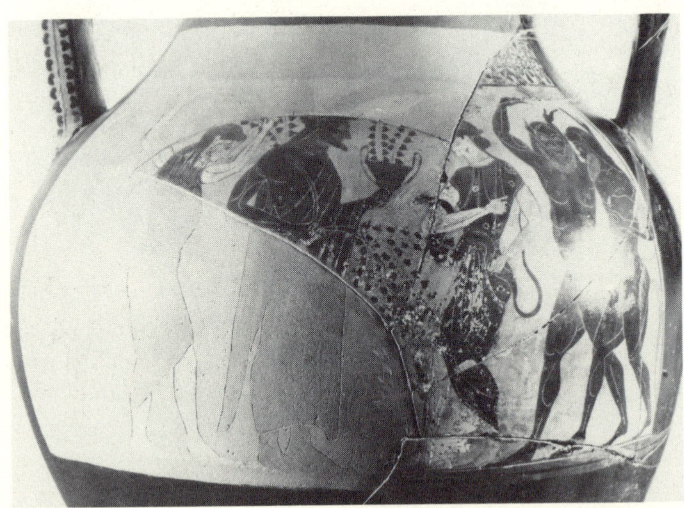

9. FF 15. Budapest, Museum of Fine Arts, 50.189, amphora. Exekias. H. (with
alien foot) 59.5 cm. Photo: Museum.

10. FF 15, detail of illus. 9. Photo: Museum.

11. Exekias, funerary plaque with frontal-faced mourner. Berlin, Staatliche Museen, F 1818 A. Preserved H. 8.5 in. Photo: Jutta Tietz-Glagow.

12. FF 80. Laon, Musée Archéologique, 37.1054, cup. Manner of the Epeleios Painter. Dm. 31.5 cm. Photo: Museum.

13. FF 80. As illus. 12.

14. FF 101. Copenhagen, National Museum, Chr. VIII 323, neck-amphora. The Tyrrhenian Group, the Prometheus Painter. H. 41.5 cm. Photo: Museum.

15. FF 102. As illus. 14.

16. FF 103. Munich, Museum antiker Kleinkunst, 1431, neck-amphora. The Tyrrhenian Group. H. 41.6 cm. Photo: C.H. Krüger-Moessner.

17. FF 107. Paris, Musée du Louvre, E 876, dinos. The Painter of the Louvre E
876. H. 47 cm. Photo: Chuzeville.

18. FF 111. Munich, Museum antiker Kleinkunst, 8935, calyx-krater, frr.
Euphronios. H. picture frieze 7.8 cm. Photo: C.H. Krüger-Moessner.

19. FF 112. Leningrad, Hermitage Museum, B. 1650, psykter. Euphronios. H. 34.2 cm. Dm. max. 27 cm. Photo: Museum.

20. Caravaggio, *Bacchus, ca.* 1595. Florence, Uffizi. Photo: Istituto Centrale per il catalogo e la documentazione, Rome.

21. FF 74. Tarquinia, Museo Nazionale, RC 6843, amphora. Phintias. H. 66 cm. Photo: Arts of Mankind, courtesy of George Braziller.

22. FF 114. Paris, Musée du Louvre, G 13, cup. The Pedieus Painter. Dm. 25 cm. Photo: Chuzeville.

23. FF 95. Harvard University, Fogg Art Museum, 1925.30.129, cup. Douris. Dm. 29.4 cm. Photo: Museum, Bequest J.C. Hoppin.

24. FF 125. Boston, Museum of Fine Arts, 98.930, cup. Douris. Dm. 27.5 cm. Photo after L.D. Caskey and J.D. Beazley, *Attic Vase Paintings in the Museum of Fine Arts, Boston*, 1931-1963, iii, Pl. 72.

25. FF 191. Tarquinia, Museo Nazionale, RC 6846, cup. The Brygos Painter.
Photo: Istituto Centrale per il catalogo e la documentazione, Rome.

26. FF 136. Copenhagen, National Museum, 3880, cup. The Dokimasia Painter.
Dm. 29.3 cm. Photo: Museum.

27. FF 144. London, British Museum, B 194, amphora. Group E. H. 41.2 cm. Photo: Museum.

28. FF 145. Brussels, Musées Royaux d'Art et d'Histoire, R 318, neck-amphora. The Swing Painter. H. 36.5 cm. Photo: Museum.

29. FF 147. Munich, Museum antiker Kleinkunst, 1563, neck-amphora. Related to the Lysippides Painter. H. 46.3 cm. Photo: C.H. Krüger-Moessner.

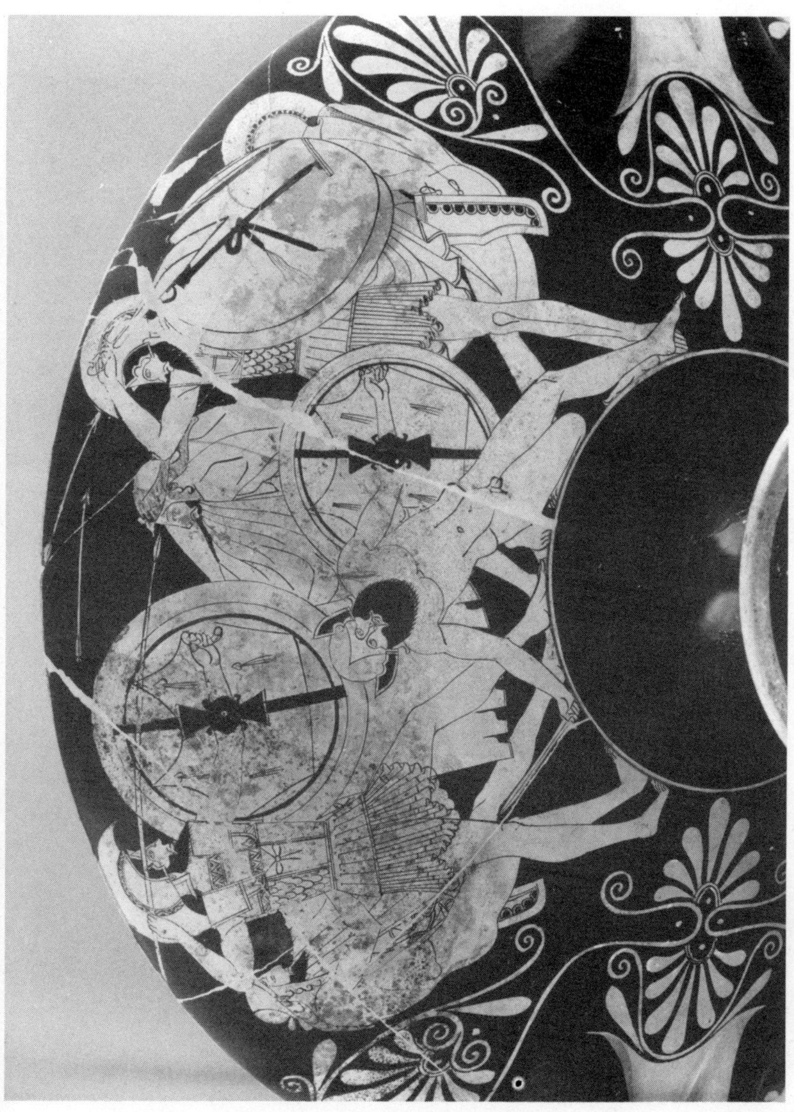

30. FF 184. Berlin, Staatliche Museen, 2288, cup. Douris. Dm. 33 cm. Photo: Jutta Tietz-Glagow.

31. FF 183. As FF 184, illus. 30.

32. FF 153. Munich, Museum antiker Kleinkunst, 1415, amphora. H. 52.5 cm. Related to the Leagros Group. Photo: C.H. Krüger-Moessner.

33. FF 165. Melbourne, National Gallery of Victoria, 1730.4, cup. The Nikosthenes Painter. Dm. 32.7 cm. Photo: Museum, Felton Bequest 1957.

34. FF 172. Bologna, Museo Civico Archeologico, PU 270, cup. The Kleophrades Painter. Dm. 27.2 cm. Photo: Museum.

35. FF 161. Rome, Museo Nazionale di Villa Giulia, cup. Oltos. H. 64.25 in. Photo: author.

36. FF 171. Naples, Museo Nazionale, 2422, hydria. The Kleophrades Painter. H. 42 cm. Photo detail after A. Furtwängler and K. Reichold, *Griechische Vasenmalerei*, i, 1904, Pl. 34.

37. FF 177. Perugia, Museo Civico, 89, cup. Onesimos. Photo after Wilhelm Klein, *Euphronios*, 1886, p. 220.

38. FF 188. Palermo, Museo Nazionale, V 659, cup. Makron. Dm. 22 cm. Photo: Soprintendenza alle antichità, Palermo.

39. FF 190. Paris, Musée du Louvre, G 154, cup. The Brygos Painter. Photo: Chuzeville.

40. FF 195. Munich, Museum antiker Kleinkunst, 1461, amphora of Panathenaic shape. Photo after JHS 25, 1905, Pl. 12 c.

41. FF 196. Rome, Musei del Vaticano, Guglielmi 34584, stamnos. The Michigan Painter. Photo after JHS 25, 1905, p. 288, fig. 24.

42. FF 197. Berlin, Staatliche Museen, F 2159, amphora. The Andokides Painter. H. with lid 58.2 cm. Photo: Jutta Tietz-Glagow.

43. FF 198. London, British Museum, E 39, cup. Douris. Dm. 27.8 cm. Photo: Museum.

44. FF 181. Berlin, Staatliche Museen, F 2287 (and frr.), cup. Douris. Photo: Jutta Tietz-Glagow.

45. FF 199-201. Munich, Museum antiker Kleinkunst, 2637, cup. Onesimos.
Photo after Wilhelm Klein, *Euphronios*, 1886, p. 284.

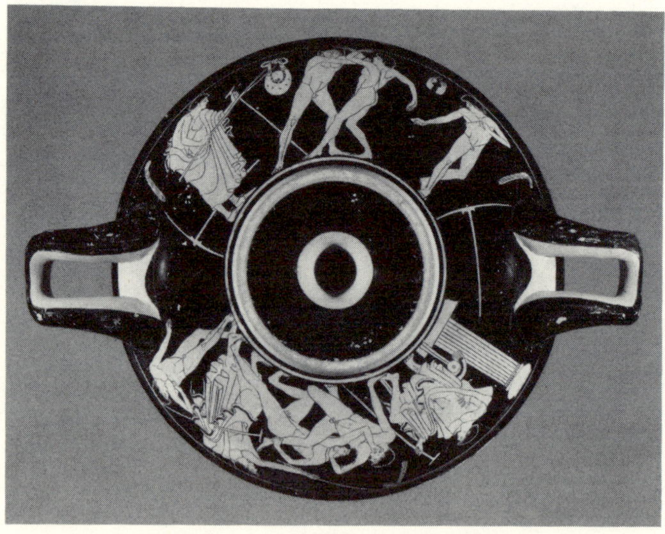

46. FF 202. Boston, Museum of Fine Arts, 1972.44, cup. Onesimos. H. 10.7 cm.
Photo: Museum, Arthur Tracy Cabot Fund.

47. FF 203. Paris, Musée du Louvre, G 291, cup. Onesimos. Photo: Chuzeville.

48. New York, Metropolitan Museum of Art, 06.1021.101, column-krater. Photo: author.

49. Rome, Museo Nazionale di Villa Giulia, 3556, hydria. The Antimenes Painter. H. 51 cm. Photo: Soprintendenza alle antichità dell'Etruria meridionale.

50. FF 166. Cambridge, Fitzwilliam Museum, GR.19.1937, cup. Wider Circle of the Nikosthenes Painter. Dm. 27.3 cm. Photo: Museum.

51. FF 207. Paris, Musée du Louvre, E 849, neck-amphora. The Tyrrhenian
Group. Photo: Chuzeville.

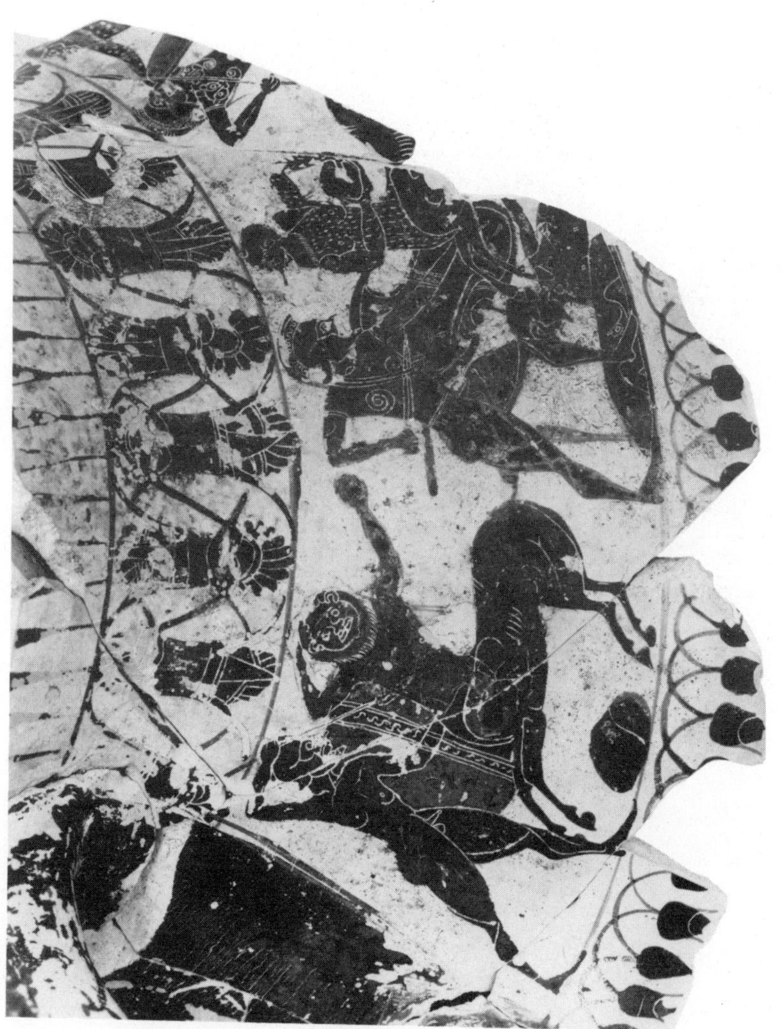

52. FF 208. Athens, Agora Museum, P 13126, amphora, fragmentary. Preserved H. *approx.* 22 cm. Photo: American School of Classical Studies at Athens, Agora Excavations.

53. FF 210. Karlsruhe, Badisches Landesmuseum, 63. 104, cup. Phintias. Dm. 38.3 cm. Photo: Museum.

54. FF 211. Florence, Museo Archeologico, 4218, skyphos, fragementary. The Kleophrades Painter. H. of largest fragment, 21 cm. Photo: Soprintendenza Archeologica per la Toscana, Firenze.

55. Paris, Musée du Louvre, CA795, relief pithos. Perseus and hippomorphic Medusa. Photo: Chuzeville.

56. FF 217 (Muse) and 219 (Dionysos). Florence, Museo Archeologico, 4209, volute-krater, the François Vase. Kleitias. H. 66 cm. Photo after A. Furtwängler and K. Reichold, *Griechische Vasenmalerei*, i, 1904, Pll. 1-2.

57. FF 216. London, British Museum, 1971.11-1.1, dinos. H. with stand 71 cm. Photo: British Museum.

58. FF 220. Boulogne-sur-Mer, Musée Communal, 559, cup. Dm. 34.5 cm. Photo: Museum.

59. FF 39. Paris, Bibliothèque Nationale, Cabinet des Médailles, 258, oinochoe.
Nikosthenic Workshop, VIII. Photo: Giraudon/Art Resource NY.

60. FF 40. Munich, Museum antiker Kleinkunst, 2088, cup. Photo: C.H. Krüger-Moessner.

61. FF 41. As FF 40, Illus. 60.

62. FF 83. Munich, Museum antiker Kleinkunst, 8732, pointed amphora. The Kleophrades Painter. H. 22 in. Photo: C.H. Krüger-Moessner.

63. FF 84. Paris, Musée du Louvre, G 196, amphora. The Troilos Painter. Photo: Chuzeville.

64. FF 110. Rome, Musei del Vaticano, 17752, hydria. Euthymides. Photo: Alinari/Art Resource NY.

65. FF 122. London, British Museum, E 64, cup. The Ashby Painter.
Photo: Museum.

66. FF 134. Leipzig, Karl-Marx-Universität, T 3367, cup. H. 36.5 cm. Makron.
Photo: Collection.

67. FF 131. Florence, Museo Archeologico, 10 B 180, cup. The Antiphon Painter. Photo: Soprintendenza alle antichità, Firenze.

68. Andrea del Castagno, *The Vision of St. Jerome*, fresco. *Ca.* 1455. Florence, SS. Annunziata. Photo: Alinari.

69. FF 218. Munich, Museum antiker Kleinkunst, 8738, stamnos. The Berlin Painter. Photo: C.H. Krüger-Moessner.

70. FF 224. Paris, Musée du Louvre, G 199, neck-amphora. The Berlin Painter. Photo: Chuzeville.

71. FF 225. London, British Museum,
E 513, oinochoe. The Berlin Painter.
Photo: Museum.

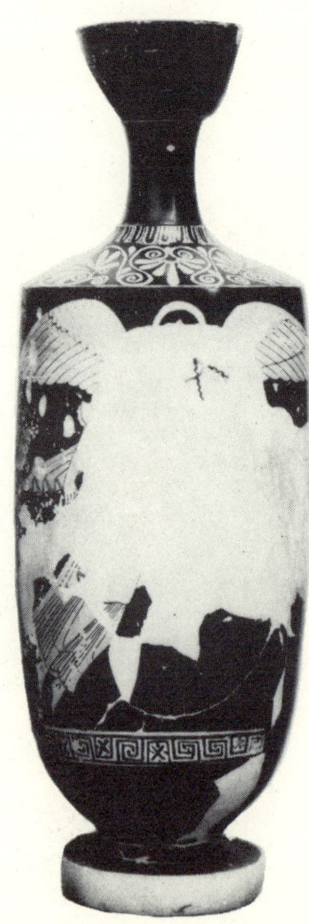

72. FF 226. Palermo, Museo Nazionale, V 670, lekythos. The Berlin Painter. H.
35.5 cm. Photo: Soprintendenza alle antichità, Palermo.

73. FF 230. As FF 191, Illus. 25.

74. FF 1. New York, Metropolitan Museum of Art, 26.49, aryballos. H. 8.50 cm. Nearchos. Photo: author.

75. FF 37. Berlin, DDR, Staatliche Museen, F 1671, neck-amphora. The BMN
Painter, Nikosthenic Workshop. Photo: Museum.

76. FF 38. As FF 37, illus. 75.

77. FF 54. San Simeon, California, Hearst Collection, 5516, neck-amphora. Photo: Collection.

78. FF 55. As FF 54, illus. 77.

79. FF 70. Copenhagen, National Museum, 10702, cup, fr. H. 9 cm. Photo: Museum.

80. FF 234. London, British Museum, B 177, amphora. Photo: Museum.

81. FF 249. Berlin, Staatliche Museen, F 2294, cup. The Foundry Painter. Dm. 30.5. cm. Photo: Bildarchiv Foto Marburg/ Art Resource NY.

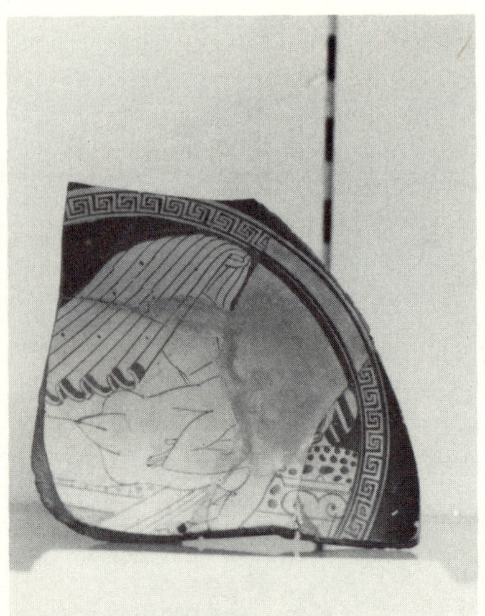

82. FF 228. New York, Metropolitan Museum of Art, 19.182.32, cup, fr. The Eucharides Painter. Photo: author.

83. FF 231. Paris, Musée du Louvre, G 282 and frr., cup, fr. Douris. Photo: Chuzeville.

84. FF 221 (Athena) and 222 (Zeus). Richmond, Virginia Museum of Fine Arts, 60.23, amphora. Group E. H. 42.5 cm. Photo: Museum.

85. London, British Museum, B 49, neck-amphora. Photo: Museum.

86. FF 223. Munich, Museum antiker Kleinkunst, 1540, neck-amphora. The Kleophrades Painter. H. 41.5 cm. Photo: C.H. Krüger-Moessner.

87. London, British Museum, E 168, hydria. Photo: Museum.

YVONNE KORSHAK

88. FF 236. Toronto, Royal Ontario Museum, 926.19.2, neck-amphora. H. 49.2 cm. Photo: Museum.

89. FF 237 (warrior in quadriga) and 238 (standing warrior). Cleveland, Museum of Art, 75.1, hydria. H. 17 in. Photo: Museum, J.H. Wade Fund.

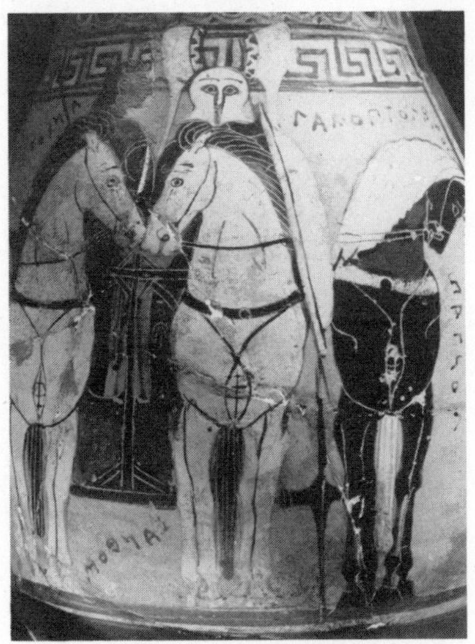

90. Paris, Musée du Louvre, E 648, olpe, Corinthian. Photo: Chuzeville.

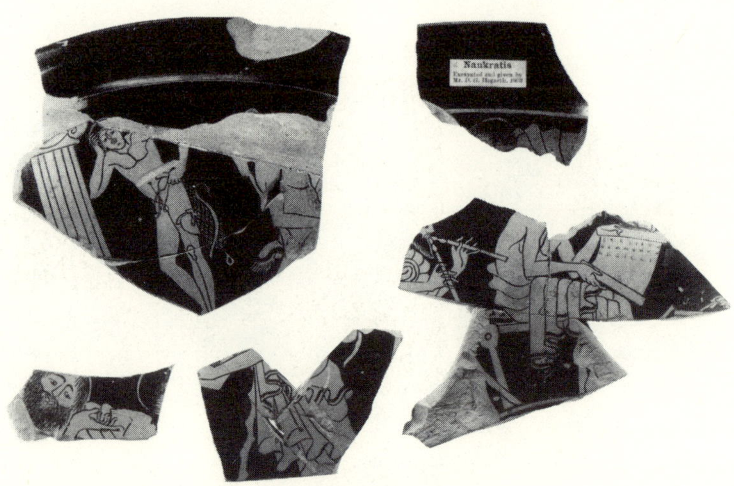

91. FF 243 (bearded man) and FF 244 (leaning youth). Oxford, Ashmolean Museum, G 138, 3, 5, 11 and frr. Onesimos. Photo: Museum.

92. FF 253. Paris, Musée du Louvre, G 333, lekythos. The Cage Painter. Photo: Chuzeville.

93. FF 246. Rome, Musei del Vaticano, 16545, cup. Douris. Dm. 30 cm. Photo: Alinari/Art Resource NY.

94. FF 129 (youth, tondo) and 247 (bearded man, bottom). Paris, Musée du Louvre, G 138, cup. The Triptolemos Painter. Photo: Chuzeville.

95. Cleveland, Museum of Art, 78.59, lekythos. Attributed to Douris.
H. 37.9 cm. Photo: Museum, the J.H. Wade Fund.